# RESEARCH DESIGN FOR THE TESTING OF INTERSTATE 10 CORRIDOR

# PREHISTORIC AND HISTORIC ARCHAEOLOGICAL REMAINS

# BETWEEN INTERSTATE 17 AND 30TH DRIVE

# (GROUP II, LAS COLINAS)

by
David A. Gregory
and
Thomas R. McGuire

Cultural Resource Management Division
Arizona State Museum
University of Arizona

September 1982

Archaeological Series No. 157

# CONTENTS

# FIGURES

# TABLES

# PREFACE

This volume contains the research design that was constructed to guide the testing of historic and prehistoric resources within the proposed Interstate 10 corridor between Interstate 17 and 30th Drive, Phoenix, Arizona, and which was submitted to the Arizona Department of Transportation in April of 1980. The testing program was carried out between December 10, 1980, and February 6, 1981, under the direction of Katharina J. Schreiber of the Arizona State Museum, University of Arizona. The results of that testing program have now been published (Schreiber, McCarthy, and Byrd 1981). Although published in an order the reverse of what would have been desirable, the research design and the testing report should be seen as companion volumes. Also available is the final report on the 1968 excavations at the feature known as Mound 8, whichlies within the freeway corridor (Hammack and Sullivan 1981). This report had not been published when the research design for the testing program was prepared. Because some sections of the research design were included in the testing report, and because the then unpublished data from Mound 8 were drawn upon substantially in the preparation of the research design, there is unavoidable redundancy among the three publications. The decision to publish the research design in spite of this redundancy was made for the reasons given below.

It is now the policy of the Cultural Resource Management Division to publish the research designs for all major research projects. These designs serve as explicit statements of how particular research efforts were originally conceived, and serve as baselines against which the results of the testing programs may be assessed. In combination with the report on the testing program, this document provides, therefore, a basis for assessing the efficacy of the original design for research and the success of the testing program in achieving the stated research goals of the project. The temptation to revise and augment the research design was strong, for it would have been possible, after the passage of time, and upon reflection, to rewrite unclear sections, to add references missed or omitted in the original, and to clean up the work prior to publication. The temptation has been resisted. Such a modified document would not impart a true impression of the nature of research designs in general, it would not accurately present the research design as originally conceived, and it would not provide a basis for a fair assessment of the results of the testing program.

Because the central importance of research designs in effectively structuring research efforts has been recognized and accepted within the discipline, and because research designs are now required in most contract projects, they have become an increasingly frequent form of expression for archaeologists. Many research designs remain unpublished, however, and there is consequently a paucity of available examples of the form for use as general models. In addition, it is often the case that materials collected in the process of constructing particular research designs have relevance beyond the specific context for which the design was created. If unublished, such potentially useful information also remains generally unavailable to both the professional and lay communities. We believe that the research design presented here well illustrates the fact that a substantial amount of useful information can be collected, analyzed, and presented in the research design stage of a project. Thomas McGuire's examination of the relevant historical records, for example, provided a wealth of quite specific information concerning the history and potential effects of urban and agricultural development on archaeological sites in the Phoenix area, as well as on the postoccupational processes affecting prehistoric sites. By applying this data to the corridor segment under consideration, I was able to reconstruct a history of postoccupational processes for that portion of the Las Colinas site lying within the corridor, and was able to develop legitimate expectations about the condition of any remaining prehistoric deposits. Data of this kind clearly have relevance beyond the concerns of the Papago Freeway project. Although the information available for this segment of the I-10 corridor was particularly rich, similar approaches in different situations may be expected to yield equally positive results. Thus, when viewed with a properly critical eye, the research design presented here may serve as a general model for what can be accomplished in the context of developing research designs for particular situations, and illustrates that such work can often result in more general contributions to knowledge.

The Papago Freeway project has had a long, complicated, and controversial history, especially with respect to the treatment of the cultural resources in the project area. We believe that much of the controversy and many of the misunderstandings have resulted from a lack of available information regarding the character of the resources in question. Whether or not one agrees with the direction taken in this document, the data presented here should provide a basis upon which both professionals and laymen can build better informed opinions.

For these reasons, and despite some overlap with the material contained in previously published reports, the document that follows is essentially the one submitted originally to the Arizona Department of Transportation. Minor editorial changes have been made and typophoical errors have, of course, been corrected.

We would like to thank many individuals who have contributed in various ways to the writing of this research design.

Richard Ervin performed ably as our research assistant, helping with everything from basic archival research to the paste-up of photographs.

The Department of Anthropology, Arizona State University, provided archival data, including many of the photographs taken by Frank Midvale and included in this document. Special thanks are due Minnabell Laughlin, who graciously assisted in the location and use of these materials.

Richard Pinkerton and Rod Myers of the Photogrammetry Section of the Arizona Department of Transportation aided in locating several of the aerial photographs reproduced here. Raul Cordova of the Greenwood Cemetery maintenancestaff provided useful information concerning the distribution of subsurface materials in the area east of Mound 7. Laurens C. Hammack gave freely of his time in discussing his 1968 work at Mound 8 and made helpful comments and suggestions. We thank all of these individuals for their assistance.

Two people were particularly resonant sounding boards and sources of good counsel. David R. Wilcox provided data on the site of Los Hornos and was a continual source of ideas and advice. Lynn Teague participated in the almost daily discussions carried on during the writing of this document and provided moral and administrative support. We greatly appreciate the important contribution of these colleagues.

Teague, Wilcox, Susan Brew, Paul Fish, Suzanne Fish, Bruce Huckell, Patricia Crown, Keith Kintigh, Michael B. Schiffer, and R. Gwinn Vivian all read and made useful comments on various portions of the research design or otherwise made their expertise available.

Charles Sternberg did his usual excellent job of drafting the figures included here. To Susan Brew, Maria Abdin, Sue Ruiz, and Esther Walks, who typed portions of the manuscript, we are grateful. The manuscript has benefitted from the editorial skills of Rose Houk and Benjamin Smith, and Houk was also responsible for the task of entering the material into the computer. Carol Heathington McCarthy coded the manuscript for typesetting and prepared the layout. Our sincere appreciation goes to these individuals for their careful work.

Finally, we would like to take this opportunity to correct several serious omissions from the original acknowledgements of the research design. James Ayres, then State Historic Preservation Officer, and Frank Fryman, Assistant State Historic Preservation Officer, provided valuable insights, suggestions, data, and guidance during the preparation of the research design. Along with Ayres and Fryman, Thomas Willett and David Bender, both of the Federal Highways Administration, and William Ross and James Dorre, of the Arizona Department of Transportation, participated in the long and sometimes arduous meetings that took place while the document was being written. Their commitment to, and genuine interest in, the proper treatment of cultural resources, as well as their unflagging good will, made our task much easier and more rewarding than it might otherwise have been. Their substantial contribution is gratefully acknowledged.

Any errors in fact or logic contained in this document are solely the responsibility of the authors.

David A. Gregory
Tucson, Arizona
June 1982

# ABSTRACT

This report deals with the proposed testing of prehistoric and historic archaeological resources within the Interstate 10 (I-10) corridor between Interstate 17 and 30th Drive (Group II, Las Colinas) in Phoenix, Arizona. The historic and prehistoric resources are dealt with in separate sections of the research design.

The research design dealing with historic resources documents the search for evidence bearing on the possible existence, character, location, and condition of any subsurface historic remains within the pertinent segment of the I-10 corridor. This research shows that for much of its recorded history the corridor segment area consisted of sparsely settled agricultural land.

With the exception of several historic canal segments and a house and associated well, no evidence for the possible existence of undocumented historic resources was discovered. No surface indications of the house and well or the canal segments have been observed during the several surface surveys of the corridor. Because of the scale and accuracy of the maps from which the information was derived, it is impossible to determine precisely the former location of the house and well. Thus it is not possible to derive a specific testing program to deal with these features. Their approximate location has been noted, and the possibility of encountering the remains of the house and well has been considered in conjunction with the testing of the prehistoric resources. The approximate position and alignment of the canal segments may be plotted. It is likely that parts of these segments will be encountered during the testing for prehistoric resources, and this probability has been considered in the context of that testing. No testing specifically directed at these historic canal segments is proposed.

The portion of the research design dealing with the prehistoric resources first addresses several preliminary research questions that were employed to guide the background research. Data relating to the original nature and extent of Las Colinas, to the relationship of the site to the I-10 corridor, and to the postoccupational processes that have affected the site are reviewed and discussed. For the purposes of this and subsequent discussions, the corridor is divided into six sub-areas.

It is shown that Las Colinas was a large Hohokam site that probably once covered slightly less than 2 square miles.

The site once contained numerous features, including several platform mounds, trash mounds, houseblocks, pit houses, borrow pits, cremations, inhumations, and possibly a ballcourt. These features were distributed in a roughly linear fashion along an approximately north-south axis. The site appears to have been occupied primarily during the Classic period (A.D. 1150 to 1450), but there is some evidence for earlier occupations. The I-10 corridor cuts the former extent of the site in an east-west direction, subsuming the feature known as Mound 8 and passing slightly north of the feature designated Mound 7. The principal postoccupational processes that have affected Las Colinas include cultivation of the land and associated activities, and the construction of houses, buildings and roads. Most of the major features at the site had been substantially disturbed or destroyed by 1930. The postoccupational processes occurring within the I-10 corridor mirror those experienced by the site as a whole. All but one of the corridor sub-areas had been brought under cultivation by 1889, and parts of the area were still being farmed through the 1950s and even the 1960s. Several early residences associated with the agricultural use of the area were constructed within or near the corridor, but the development of the bulk of the corridor area for residential purposes did not occur until the 1950s and even the 1960s. Even today, substantial portions of the corridor segment under consideration remain as open lots and fields.

A testing program based on the information from the preliminary research is presented. Additional research questions are generated to guide the proposed testing, and these questions are related to several current issues in Hohokam archaeology. The methodology to be employed for the testing is outlined and discussed. The techniques to be used include remote sensing (Subsurface Interface Radar), backhoe trenching, and some hand excavation. The specific combinations of these techniques to be used in each of the corridor sub-areas are presented and discussed. These combinations of techniques are tailored to the existing information for each sub-area and to the managerial and scientific goals of the proposed testing. The kinds of data to be collected and the modes of analysis to be employed in processing those data are presented. A plan of work is included in the Appendix.

# Chapter 1
# INTRODUCTION

The following research design deals with the proposed testing of prehistoric and historic archaeological remains within that portion of the Interstate 10 corridor lying west of Interstate 17 and east of 30th Drive in Phoenix, Arizona.

## Purposes and Goals of the Testing Program

At the present time (spring 1980) a variety of options are still open with respect to the specific nature of construction to be employed in the I-10 corridor segment under consideration. In order to complete the consultation process contained in 36 CFR 800, the Federal Highway Administration official in charge and the State Historic Preservation Officer have determined that additional information is necessary to evaluate the existing construction options with respect to their possible impacts on remaining historic and prehistoric resources within the corridor. Since the available information regarding historic and prehistoric resources differs considerably, each type of resource will be treated differently in this report.

## Historic Resources

Before this study, no research had been accomplished on the possible presence, nature, and condition of subsurface historic remains within this segment of the corridor. Consequently, it is necessary to provide sufficient information concerning any historic archaeological resources so that eligibility and effect determinations may be made, and so that appropriate decisions may be made regarding mitigation of impacts to the historic resources. With respect to historic remains, the preparation of the research design for the proposed testing has included the basic archival and documentary research required to establish the possible existence, character, and condition of any subsurface historic remains within the corridor. In light of this research, the need for any field testing is evaluated and recommendations are made.

## Prehistoric Resources

The situation with respect to prehistoric resources is quite different. Found within the corridor is the feature designated Mound 8, a part of the archaeological site of Las Colinas (AZ T:12:10, ASM). Mound 8 was the focus of intensive investigation by the Arizona State Museum in 1968 (Hammack 1969). The portion of this site within the corridor has been determined eligible for the National Register of Historic Places under criteria C and D.

The pertinent management decision to be made regarding the prehistoric remains within the corridor is to reasonably determine the distribution and character of remaining subsurface resources away from the immediate area of Mound 8. The evaluation of existing construction options and, therefore, in part the development of an avoidance and mitigation plan, is contingent on the definition of these limits. To provide the required managerial information, it is necessary to determine the probable distribution, nature, and condition of subsurface prehistoric remains that may exist within the corridor. This does not mean that the precise location of every feature and deposit of materials in the corridor must be established; it does mean that the relative distribution of remains must be reasonably estimated.

The simple determination of the presence or absence of prehistoric features and materials is not sufficient, however, as a goal of scientific research. The fact that the testing will be quite limited in scope and will not in any way constitute "data recovery" in the formal sense of the term does not exempt the testing program from the responsibility of dealing adequately with the data that will, in fact, result. Even if no artifacts were recovered during testing, the recorded absence of materials would constitute archaeological data potentially relevant to an understanding of prehistory.

The general managerial goals must, therefore, be meshed with a well-considered program of research that may be expected to produce specific and useful scientific information. The scientific utility of the data that may result from the testing program depends in turn on the questions constructed to guide the investigation. Thus, while the managerial goals of the testing program are fairly straightforward, the scientific and archaeological concerns are fairly complex. These concerns are embodied in the research questions generated in the course of preparing this research design. These questions and the body of information necessary to understand them are presented below.

There exists also a shared managerial and scientific goal: that of providing the required information for both concerns while keeping any disturbance to existing resources at a minimum. This consideration has weighed heavily in all decisions regarding the testing program. It is reflected specifically in several aspects of the proposed testing.

# Chapter 2

# HISTORIC RESOURCES

by Thomas R. McGuire

The Interstate 10 corridor west of I-17 now contains few of the remnants of the developing urban system of metropolitan Phoenix. Before the Arizona Department of Transportation acquired the corridor, it was shared by light industry and residential subdivisions. As this landscape evolved after World War II, scattered reminders of an earlier phase in the historic growth of Phoenix could still be seen. Well outside the original Phoenix townsite, and until 1959 even outside the boundaries of the incorporated city, the lands along the proposed corridor were prime agricultural tracts. The "taming of the Salt," a phrase used frequently in the public relations literature of the Salt River Project, brought irrigation water to the western lands of the valley in the 1870s. Settlement and growth of Phoenix was predicated on agricultural lands such as these, and the early homesteaders worked hard to fulfill this initial promise. So crucial to the survival and expansion of the town, the activities once performed on these farmlands ironically leave few historical remains. Large tracts were put under the plow; houses, barns, and the mundane structures of a farming economy were dispersed over the landscape. Canals and laterals were dug into the valley, and an occasional well sunk to the underlying aquifer. By design, these human alterations took up as little space as possible, leaving the bulk of the land free for crops. By chance, the proposed I-10 corridor is superimposed on few of these dispersed and infrequent historical alterations. By chance, too, there are relatively few bodies of documentary materials that directly highlight the historical processes of settlement and growth in the narrow corridor. In short, few detailed answers can be supplied to the set of proposed research questions. Specifically, we sought answers to the following questions:

1. *Were any historic features ever constructed within the area? What was the location of these features?*
2. *What was the nature of the features?*
3. *What processes have affected the features since the time of their construction?*
4. *Do any historic features or their remnants still exist within the area? If so, what is the location, nature, and condition of these remains?*

*The documentary search revealed few unknown historic remains in the corridor area. Subsequent sections of this report will review the stages followed in this documentary search and summarize what these documents say aboutthe place of the corridor area in the growth of the Salt River Valley in historic times.*

## Known Historic Remains

Arizona State Museum's surface surveys of the corridor and the testing and excavation at Mound 8 have documented several historic remains. To the east of the mound is a section of an irrigation lateral, now apparently unused for cultivation. Near this lateral, and directly atop Mound 8, were the remnants of an adobe house with a basement dug 4 feet into the mound along with associated outbuildings. Analysis of construction style, coupled with information on dates of homesteading in the area (summarized in Table 2.1), place the date of construction for the house in the 1880s. It stood until 1956, when it was destroyed by fire. In conjunction with archaeological excavation of Mound 8 in 1968, unsystematic collection of historic artifacts from the basement of the house was carried out. The collections have been analyzed and reported by Staski (1981). Finally, a brick house, garage, and shed were built near Mound 8, fronting on 27th Avenue. These structures are still standing but are of relatively recent date. They do not appear on aerial photographs of 1936 and 1940 and were probably constructed in the 1940s.

No additional historic properties or remains were located by previous surface surveys of the corridor segment under consideration.

## Documentary History of the Corridor

In an attempt to locate information on additional historic properties in the corridor area, documentary materials from diverse sources were examined. Initially, I perused

TABLE 2.1

**Homestead Entries in and Near the I-10 Corridor**

| Township, Range | NE¼<br>NE NW SW SE | NW¼<br>NE NW SW SE | SW¼<br>NE NW SW SE | SE¼<br>NE NW SW SE | Entry |
|---|---|---|---|---|---|
| **T1N R2E**<br>Section 1 | | | | | TC 1878–1883<br>HE 1890<br>Railroad R/W 1892<br>HE 1890<br>CE 1885<br>TC 1878–1881<br>HE 1878–1883<br>HE 1884–1886<br>TC 1886–1887<br>CE 1891 |
| Section 2 | | | | | TC 1876–1878<br>CE 1890<br>CE 1880<br>TC 1878–1878<br>HE 1881<br>HE 1888 |
| Section 3 | | | | | CE 1890<br>HE 1886–1887<br>CE 1890<br>HE 1890<br>TC 1895 |
| **T2N R2E**<br>Section 34 | | | | | TC 1878–1878<br>CE 1888<br>Military Patent 1880<br>CE 1888<br>CE 1888 |
| Section 35 | | | | | TC 1885–1886<br>CE 1891<br>CE 1889<br>CE 1880<br>HE 1888<br>CE 1888 |
| Section 36 | | | | | Railroad R/W 1892<br>SRP 1902–1936 |

Key     CE    Cash entry          R/W    Right-of-Way          TC    Timber culture entry
        HE    Homestead entry     SRP    Salt River Project    ☐     On I-10 corridor

| Summary | Entry type | Cancelled | Proven | Total |
|---|---|---|---|---|
| | Homestead | 3 | 6 | 9 |
| | Timber culture | 7 | 1 | 8 |
| | Cash | 0 | 13 | 13 |

some of the voluminous property files gathered by the Arizona Department of Transportation (ADOT) in its process of acquiring the corridor lands. These files contain correspondence and legal title searches for the plots and structures in the right-of-way, but little information of historical value. ADOT was mandated only to trace ownership back to clear and uncontested title which, for the properties in the corridor, was recent. Nonetheless, an examination of these files served to establish some working temporal limits for historical research. Since about 1945, the present pattern of land use in and near the corridor has been established. In subsequent archival research, I concentrated my efforts on material covering the century prior to this contemporary period. Primary efforts in this search were directed to materials in the following locations: Maricopa County Recorder's, Assessor's, and Treasurer's offices; the General Land Office of the U.S. Bureau of Land Management, Phoenix; Arizona State Department of Archives; the Tucson and Phoenix branches of the Arizona Historical Society, the Arizona Historical Foundation and the Arizona Collection in the Arizona State University Library; the Special Collections and general shelf collections of the University of Arizona Library; the State Historic Preservation Office; and the museum of the Salt River Project. Some additional material was gathered by an employee of the firm of Cox and Cox, Attorneys, Phoenix. While the primary purpose of this search was to uncover information on the existence of unknown historic properties in the corridor area, the following summary of these various archival materials will seek to place the pertinent section of the corridor itself into the larger patterns of historic land use in the region.

## Pima-Maricopa Ethnography

Documentary and ethnographic literature on the Pima and Maricopa Indians of the Gila-Salt region is relatively rich (Ezell 1961, 1963; Spier 1933; Russell 1975; Winter 1973; Hackenberg 1962), but there are few indications that either group inhabited permanent settlements north of the Salt River in historic times, prior to the establishment of the Salt River Pima Reservation near Scottsdale. From his close examination of the diaries of travelers through the region, Ezell (1961) is able to plot the location and shifts of known settlements in the seventeenth, eighteenth, and nineteenth centuries (Figs. 2.1, 2.2, 2.3). None of these villages is found north of the Salt River, but Ezell points out that few travelers ever crossed to the north bank. John Russell Bartlett's narrative is thus important. He crossed the river on his explorations for the United States-Mexico Boundary Commission in 1852, and reports on the nature of Pima land use there. Exposed to the attacks of hostile Yavapai and Apache, the north bank was apparently occupied only temporarily for seasonal hunting and fishing.

At six o'clock this morning [July 3, 1852] we set off, the party consisting of Dr. Webb, Messrs. Thurber, Pratt, Seaton, Force, Leroux, and myself, with attendants. Lieutenant Paige, with six soldiers, also accompanied us, that officer wishing to examine the opposite bank of the Gila, as well as the lands contiguous to the Salinas, with a view of establishing a military post in the vicinity of the Pimo villages. After crossing the bed of the Gila we pursued a westerly course about eight miles to the point of a range of mountains, near which we struck the bottom-lands. We now inclined more to the north, and in about eight miles struck the Salinas, about twelve miles from its mouth, where we stopped to let the animals rest and feed. The bottom, which we crossed diagonally, is from three to four miles wide. The river we found to be from eighty to one hundred and twenty feet wide, from two to three feet deep, and both rapid and clear. In these respects it is totally different from the Gila, which, for the two hundred miles we had traversed its banks, was sluggish and muddy, a character which I think it assumes after passing the mountainous region and entering one with alluvial banks. The water is perfectly sweet, and neither brackish nor salt, as would be inferred from the name. We saw from the banks many fish in its clear waters, and caught several of the same species as those taken in the Gila. The margin of the river on both sides, for a width of three hundred feet, consists of sand and gravel, brought down by freshets when the stream overflows its banks; and from the appearance of the drift-wood lodged in the trees and bushes, it must at times be much swollen, and run with great rapidity. The second terrace or bottom-land, varies from one to four miles in width, and is exceedingly rich. As it is but little elevated above the river, it could be irrigated with ease. At present it is covered with shrubs and mezquit trees, while along the immediate margin of the stream large cotton-wood trees grow. Near by we saw the remains of several Indian wigwams, some of which seemed to have been but recently occupied. Francisco told us they were used by his people and the Pimos when they came here to fish. He also told us that two years before, when the cholera appeared among them, they abandoned their dwellings on the Gila and came here to escape the pestilence.

Owing to the intense heat, we lay by until five o'clock, and again pursued our journey up the river until dark, when, finding a little patch of poor grass, we thought best to stop for the night. Supper was got, and a good meal made from our fish. As we brought no tents, we prepared our beds on the sand.

We had not long been in when we saw a body of twelve or fifteen Indians on the river making for our camp. At first some alarm was felt, until Francisco told us that they were Pimos. They proved to be a party which had been engaged in hunting and fishing. They were a jolly set of young men, dancing and singing while they remained with us. I told them we would like a few fish for breakfast, if they would bring them in.

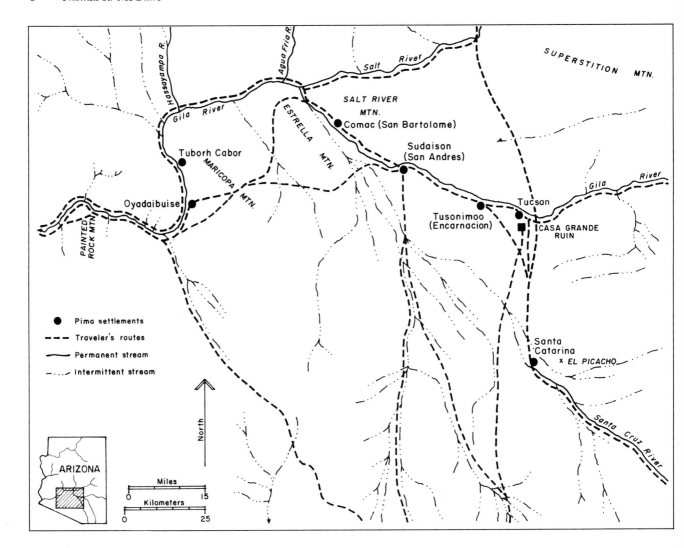

*Figure 2.1.* Travelers' routes and Pima settlements of the Jesuit period, 1694–1767 (from Ezell 1961).

With this encouragement, they took leave of us, promising to fetch us some in the morning. But instead of waiting til the morning, they returned to the camp about midnight, aroused the whole party with their noise, and wished to strike a bargain at once for their fish, a pile of which, certainly enough to last a week, they had brought us. There was no getting rid of them without making a purchase, which I accordingly did, when they left, and permitted us to get a few hours' more sleep (Bartlett 1854, Vol. 2: 240-242).

It is unlikely that the material remains of such seasonal camps could have withstood the alterations introduced by Anglo immigrants to the Salt River Valley. Beginning in the 1860s, the rich agricultural potential of the Salt and its floodplain began to be tested by these newcomers, and by 1910 much of the valley was under cultivation. This influx of settlers destroyed more than the vestiges of past Pima settlements and camps, however. Writing his annual report to the Commissioner of Indian Affairs in 1900, Agent Elwood Hadley of the Pima Agency at Sacaton surveys this social destruction, wrought by 30 years of Anglo settlement and cultivation in the Salt-Gila region:

> During the past few years this water, their one resource, their very life, has been taken from them, and they are, perforce, lapsing into indolence, misery, and vice. The waters of the Gila River have been diverted by white settlers above them and, instead of waving fields of green in the summer, there is nothing now to be seen but the dry, parched earth. Year after year they have tried in vain to mature their crops with the insufficient quantity of water left them, and now, on account of the unprecedented drought which has prevailed throughout the country during all the past year, they have practically no water at all. A few, located at points where the water under the bed of the river rises to the surface can still get partial crops; some make a bare living by hauling or doing other work when they are fortunate enough to find any to do. The greater number must soon become more or less dependent upon charity (Hadley 1900: 195).

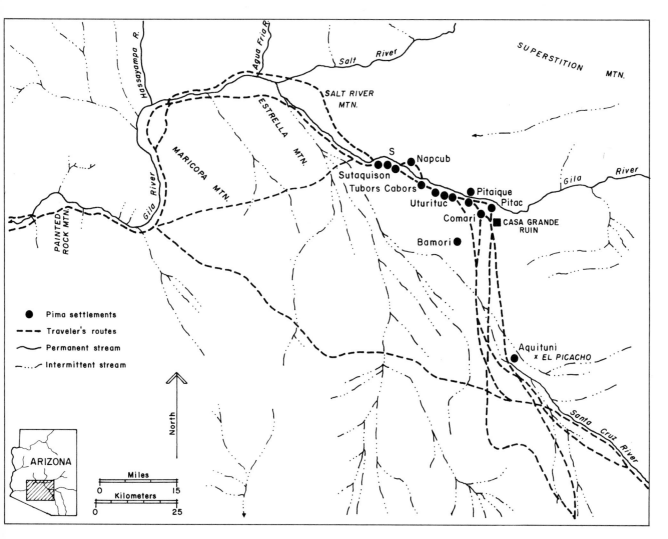

*Figure 2.2.* Travelers' routes and Pima settlements of the Franciscan period, 1768–1795 (from Ezell 1961).

## Histories of Phoenix Settlement

The story of Anglo settlement in the Salt River Valley has been recounted in great detail in several works, most notably Farish (1918, Vol. 4: 69-273), Barney (1933), Mawn (1977), and Frazer (1959). Frazer's study of historical geography provides an overview of the process of urban expansion and changing land values, but it has little useful detail on small sections of the valley and no relevant information on the zone in and near the I-10 corridor. Farish, Barney, and Mawn focus their attention on the political history of the original Phoenix townsite in Section 8, T1N R3E. The story is an engrossing one of political intrigue and economic speculation, but, once again, the area on the highway corridor remained outside the mainstream of these events, and thus receives little direct attention.

Geoffrey Mawn (1977: 207) has concisely summarized the earliest years of settlement in the Salt River Valley:

During the late 1860s a succession of mineral discoveries in Arizona attracted groups of prospectors, farmers, and businessmen to the newly created territory. Some settled in the old pueblo of Tucson, while many fanned out to the mining districts and founded Prescott, Wickenburg, and other towns. Still others, attracted by markets at Camp McDowell and in the surrounding mines, entered the broad valley of the Salt and established a small agricultural settlement called Phoenix. Here, as elsewhere in the territory, a small group of speculators in land and trade played a crucial role in urban development. As early as 1867 they began promoting the area, with a view of building the economic base of the valley upon irrigated agriculture. This was unique because most of the new urban centers in the territory had sprung up in mining regions. In time, a dominant group, headed by John T. Alsap, a local politician and farmer, chose a central point in the valley for a townsite, and guided the young town of Phoenix to its confirmation as a legal entity.

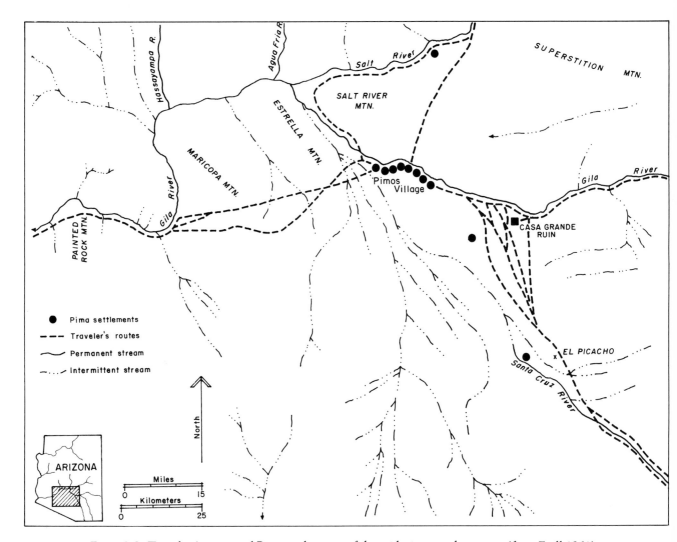

*Figure 2.3.* Travelers' routes and Pima settlements of the mid-nineteenth century (from Ezell 1961).

With ready markets for crops at Fort McDowell and Wickenburg, the broad stretch of the Salt River Valley thus proved attractive to farmers. Selection of a townsite was more difficult, however. By 1870, the dispersed farmers in the valley—some 115 Mexicans and 125 Anglos (Mawn 1977: 214)—felt the need to designate a permanent site as a "trading center for the exchange of goods and services" (Mawn 1977: 215). Several locations were proposed by different factions, each seeking the economic boon of a site on lands they already owned. A strong contender for the location was the McKinnie-Carpenter quarter-section, upon which these two Republicans operated a saloon (Fig. 2.4). Mawn recounts the immediate opposition to this proposal (Mawn 1977: 216-217):

> Another group of farmers, principally Democrats, led by Gray, Montgomery and the Starar brothers, objected to the choice of the McKinnie-Carpenter tract, because it was littered with mounds of ancient Indian ruins. They demanded that the townsite be located on level ground free of ruins and easy to clear of mesquite

and greasewood. This would reduce the expense of subdividing lots and would maximize profits. They also opposed the Hellings millsite, or any other site in the original settlement, and urged that the town be placed on unoccupied land, so all interested parties would have an equal opportunity for speculative investment. Because these farmers claimed property below the Phoenix settlement, they naturally wanted the new town located near their lands.

The alternative site, later named the "original townsite," eventually won approval, as Mawn recounts (1977: 218):

> The proposed townsite had certain advantages. It was more than a mile north of the river and on ground above the seasonal floodplain. It also lay in the geographical center of the valley, an important factor in the community's future as an urban center. The gradual, sloping contour of the land facilitated quick construction of buildings, easy maintenance of streets, and a natural drainage. Few vestiges of prehistoric ruins marred the landscape, and the only thick mesquite in the area was on the western part of the site.

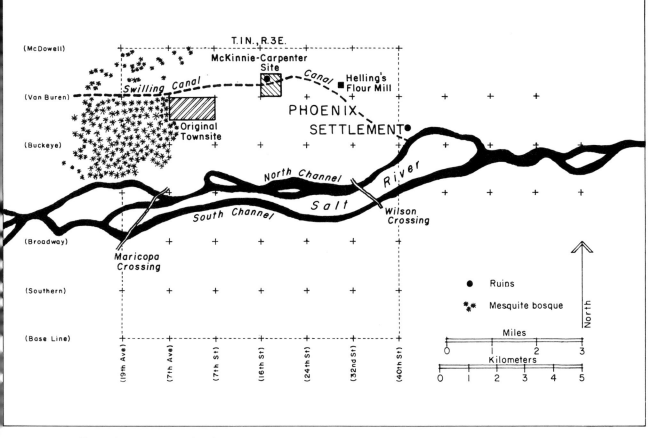

*Figure 2.4.* Features of early settlement in the Phoenix area (from Mawn 1977 and Bufkin 1977).

For the same reasons that this site was selected, the lands under the present I-10 corridor would have been unattractive. Prehistoric ruins and dense mesquite dominated the landscape of Sections 1 and 2, T2N R2E. Nonetheless, these sections, surveyed in 1867, on the main road between Wickenburg and Phoenix and close enough to the new townsite to afford some of the amenities of commerce and villages, were quickly homesteaded and brought under cultivation.

## Land Surveys and Homesteads

From their initial monument at the junction of the Gila and Salt rivers, William Pierce and Wilfred Ingalls surveyed the Salt River Valley in 1867 and 1868. The General Land Office in Phoenix retains the original plats, along with the handwritten field notes of these surveys. Following their general instructions, the surveyors recorded on these plats significant geographic features, existing roads, dominant vegetation types, and soil qualities. Through the Salt River region their task was uncomplicated: the terrain was easy, and by 1868 few human alterations of the landscape had yet occurred. The resulting plats of T1N R2E and T2N R2E (Figs. 2.5 and 2.6) show dense growths of mesquite on

the level land north of the river. The lower wagon road from Fort McDowell to Wickenburg skirts these mesquite thickets through sections of these townships. Pressed to complete their mapping of lands around the new Phoenix settlement, the surveyors did not consistently record prehistoric features on these plats.

Information on the subsequent occupation of the valley is contained in the Historical Indices of the General Land Office (GLO). Arranged by township, these indices record the transfer of federal property into private, state, or county ownership. Once the parcels go out of federal hands, the GLO keeps no record on further transactions. Thus these indices provide information on the initial homesteaders and, occasionally, on the false starts and unproved land patents. In the six sections in the I-10 corridor area, there were indeed some false starts. Some of these false starts are illustrated on a map compiled by historian James M. Barney in 1931 (Fig. 2.7). Table 2.1, based on information obtained from the General Land Office, summarizes the early attempts to turn these sections into homesteads and farms. Not surprisingly, entries under the Timber Culture Act were seldom retained. Discussing the operation of this legislation in New Mexico, Victor Westphall (1965: 72) could be speaking of the Salt River Valley as well:

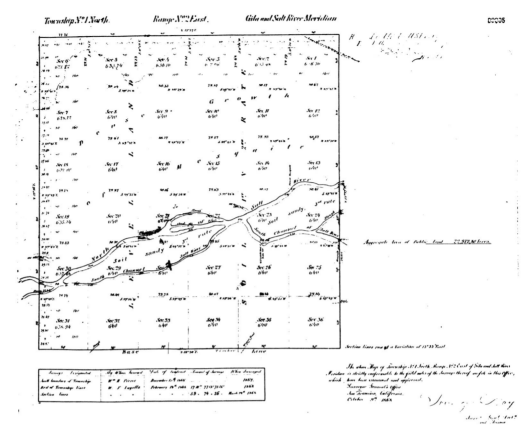

Figure 2.5. 1868 survey plat, T1N R2E.

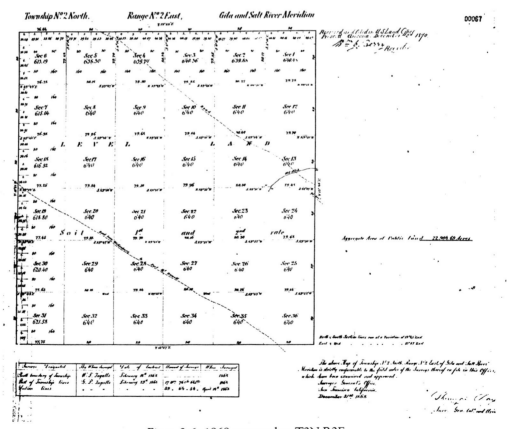

Figure 2.6. 1868 survey plat, T2N R2E.

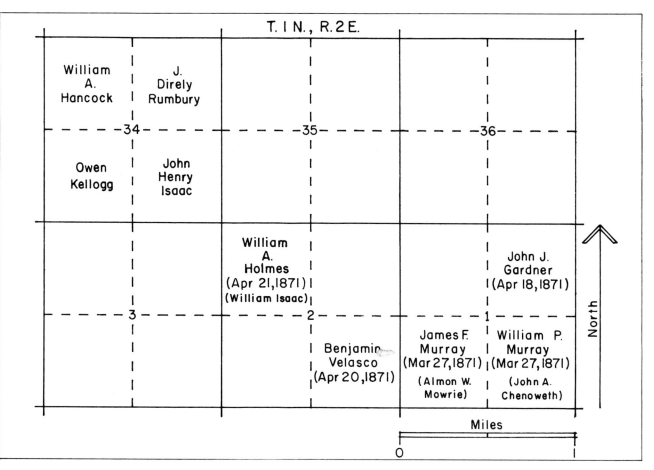

*Figure 2.7.* Barney's map of early homestead entries in the Salt River Valley (1931).

The Timber Culture Acts were "in substance, a subsidy paid in lands to encourage the planting and culture of timber." They were in operation from 1873 until their final repeal in 1891. They were a mistake in arid New Mexico. Except in rare instances it was impossible to comply with the law since nature controlled the balance here. Where there were trees, timber-culture was illegal. Where there were no trees, none were destined to grow without irrigation, and irrigated land was more valuable for crops than for trees.

It is perhaps more surprising that cash entries outnumbered homestead entries in these sections. Westphall addresses a similar finding in New Mexico (1965: 66):

Why would settlers buy land when free land was available through homesteading? There is no single answer to this question. An obvious answer is that a homesteader could secure additional land, through preemption [cash entry], after completing a homestead entry by means of a five-year residence or by commutation to cash in six months. Many settlers did this . . . .Another answer is more unpleasant. It was easier for the unscrupulous to find a bogus entryman to stay six months on the pre-emption claim than five years on a homestead. . . .

For the Salt River Valley, an additional reason for the frequency of cash entries may be offered. Irrigation waters reached the sections along the I-10 corridor at an early date, with the construction of the Maricopa Canal shortly before 1870 (see discussion of Kent Decree, below). With land coming into cultivation rapidly and with ready markets for crops, farmers could expect to absorb the relatively small expense of cash entry quickly. This penchant for cash entries may likewise account for the sparseness of occupational structures in the pertinent segment of the I-10 corridor area. The five years of continuous residence necessary to prove up on a homestead entry demanded relatively substantial living quarters. Cash entries, by contrast, required no proof of long-term residence. Indeed, several of the cash entries in the vicinity of the I-10 corridor belonged to owners of proven homesteads on adjacent parcels. In all probability, then, such cash entry lands contained no evidence of actual occupation.

The names of these original patent-holders must be uncovered by a somewhat tedious process. On the historical indices, patent numbers and dates of filing are recorded, along with legal descriptions of the tract. From this information, the microfiched pages of the original patent books can then be searched, and the names of the homesteaders obtained (Fig. 2.8). No additional biographical data are contained in the patent books, however. The utility of the General Land Office records is thus limited, but they do provide a necessary first step in tracing subsequent land transactions among private owners.

## Family Papers and Biographies

Family papers are seldom systematically collected and preserved, and the chances of uncovering such records for early inhabitants of the sparsely-settled section of the I-10 corridor under consideration were slim. Searches of libraries produced no collections for any of the known residents of the actual corridor. However, the life of Colonel William Christy, who homesteaded land just east of the corridor, has been preserved in a 14-page biography written and privately printed by his son, Lloyd B. Christy (1930). Some of the details of Christy's life shed light on the early settlement of the corridor area.

A Civil War veteran and banker from Clarke County, Iowa, Col. Christy came to the Salt River Valley in 1883, well after the initial settlement of Phoenix. His son, recalling these early years, offers reasons for the choice of a homestead on the outskirts of town (1930: 7):

> Phoenix at that time was a wide open town, every other business was a saloon with open doors where gambling devices could be viewed to entice the men from the mines or ranches with a few dollars to spend, and there were also the girl saloon singers, who in their cracked voices lured the men into the saloons. That sort of town did not seem to my father to furnish a very good influence for his three young sons, so he soon went to the country and bought from a settler a relinquishment on a 160-acre homestead and built a home away from the town and its influences. As father had to go to town each day, he bought himself a fine buggy and high-stepping team of horses. He was known as the man who drove the best rig in the Valley. Automobiles were coming into use before his death, but they never held any allure for him. His team that ran away with him at least once a week, next to his family, was his chief joy. The purchase of the farm put him into the agricultural class as well as banking. In the early days of this Valley when there were no railroads running into the Valley, there were hardly any markets for the grain and hay, which were almost the sole agricultural products raised, except the mines and the United States Military Posts. Many of the farmers were purchasing range cattle either in Sonora, Mexico, or from the ranges in Northern Arizona. The cattle were driven to Maricopa, loaded on the cars and shipped to Southern California, Colorado or Kansas and sold. I remember one Fall my father bought a bunch of cattle to pasture over the winter from a stockman near Prescott. He sent my brother George and myself with some cowboys to get them and deliver them at our farm. It usually took more than a week to make the drive to Phoenix.

Banking and land development were Christy's prime interests, however. He quickly became involved in the financial affairs of the valley (Hopkins 1950). Lloyd Christy intertwined his father's career with some of the crucial steps in the development of Phoenix.

> Father and Mr. W. J. Murphy became associated in the Valley Bank, Mr. Murphy took over the active management of the Arizona canal and then father joined with Mr. Murphy, Mr. Bennitt and Mr. Fulwiler in organizing the Arizona Improvement Company and was elected Manager of the Company. The Arizona Improvement Company was organized to purchase the controlling interests in the three irrigation canals lying South of the new Arizona Canal and the North Side of the Salt River. This was accomplished and the irrigation system on the North Side of the river were then co-ordinated and the water distributed from one office, and a Cross-Cut Canal was built connecting the highest canal (the Arizona Canal) with the other three canals, viz.: The Grand, Maricopa and Salt River Canals. A dam was built at the head of the Arizona Canal and all of the water, when the river was low, diverted into the Arizona Canal and then distributed to the other canals. This plan saved water to the consumer farmers as it saved the extreme evaporation in summer from the water running down a hot sandy river bed. This worked very well until a flood season occurred when the river washed out the plank dam at the head of the Arizona Canal and the canals were without water with worlds of it going down to the Gulf with no way to turn it into the canals. The dam was rebuilt several times when new floods occurred, and at last the Arizona Improvement Company's funds and credit were exhausted and the Court was asked to appoint a Receiver for the Company. A joint Receivership was appointed and father was one of the two appointed. The minority water right holders in the three older canals applied to the Court to determine their rights as to prior appropriation of water and from this came the famous "Kibbey decision" whose judgement is still in the law governing water distribution during times of water shortage in this Valley. It was at this time seen that a storage dam on the Salt River to impound the water during rainy seasons was deemed absolutely necessary for the future growth of the Salt River Valley, and the department of Arizona. A few men, of whom my father was one, were called together to study the problem confronting the Valley. It was decided to organize the leaders of the Valley and work out some plan whereby the storage of the flood waters of the Salt River could be accomplished (Figs. 2.9 and 2.10) (1930: 8,9).

Christy thus became a founder of the Salt River Valley Water Users' Association, precursor to the Salt River Project. He died in 1903, only a few weeks after the articles of incorporation for the association were signed.

Lloyd Christy's brief biography, while providing a personal glimpse of the man and his times, fails to answer questions about the economics of the Christy homestead near the highway corridor. Nor does it contain information

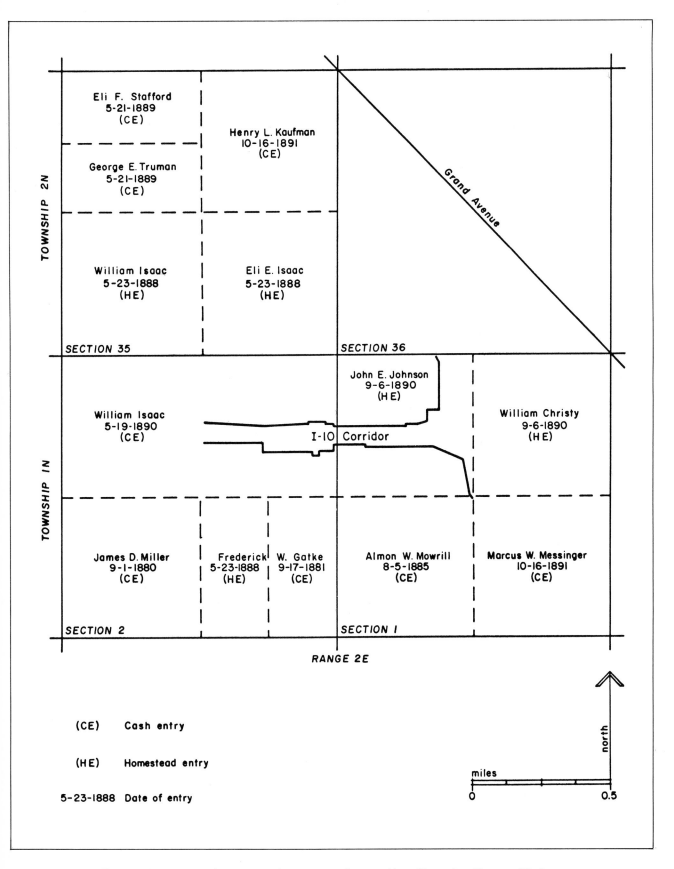

*Figure 2.8.* Homestead patents in the I-10 corridor area (from Township Historical Index, Government Land Office, Phoenix).

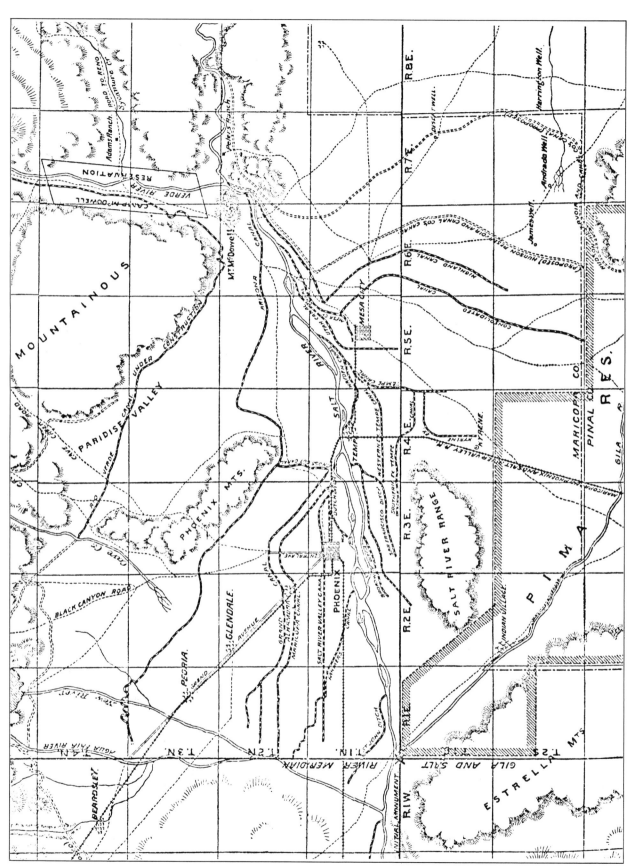

*Figure 2.9. Proposed and existing canals in the Salt River Valley, 1897 (from Davis 1897).*

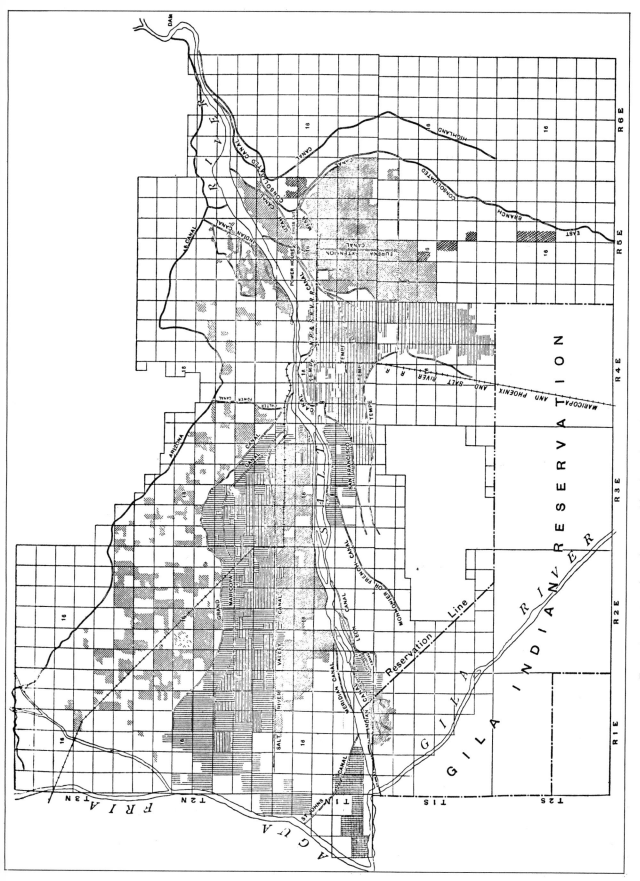

*Figure 2.10.* Canals and irrigated lands in the Salt River Valley, 1903 (from Davis 1903).

on the fate of this homestead following Christy's death. For answers to such questions, I examined land deeds and tax assessment records for Maricopa County.

## Land Deeds and Tax Assessment Rolls

The Maricopa County Recorder's Office retains records of virtually all land transactions within the county. Use of these microfilmed materials for title searches is somewhat cumbersome, however. Armed with the names of the original homesteaders, the researcher must first examine the "grantor" film, arranged alphabetically by year. Listed on the film are the names of grantor and grantee, date of the transaction, and the numbered deed book which contains the actual deed. A similar "grantee" film contains the same information, but is alphabetized by the name of the purchaser, not the seller. Once a transaction is located on the film, the actual deed must then be examined, on separate films. Deeds contain full information on the legal description of the property, names of seller and buyer, and remuneration. However, none of the deeds I examined contained information on improvements for these properties. Thus they were of little help in uncovering new information concerning historic properties in the corridor.

Despite these limitations, the deed records reveal some of the expansive activities of William Isaac, John E. Johnson, and William Christy, the three settlers along the northern halves of Sections 1 and 2, T1N R2E. William Isaac acquired a portion of Section 29, in T2N R2E in 1883 and a homestead certificate for 160 acres of Section 23 of T2N R2E in 1890. Added to his holdings in the vicinity of the I-10 corridor, Isaac thus laid claim to more than 640 acres of valley land between 1883 and 1890. John E. Johnson held a homestead entry on the NW ¼ of Section 1, T1N R2E, but he quickly acquired the holdings of three other individuals in T1N R2E. Finally, William Christy paid Marcus W. Messinger and his wife Mary $16,000 on August 23, 1892 for the 160 acres of land abutting the original Christy homestead in Section 1, T1N R2E. Thus, Christy came to own the eastern half of the section. He deeded a small strip along 19th Avenue to the Santa Fe, Prescott, and Phoenix Railroad for a right-of-way into town. Eventually the southern half of Christy's holdings would be marked off for residential subdivision, not surprisingly called "Christy's Acres."

County tax records added some information on these holdings, but, like the deed records, were of little help in isolating historic properties. Assessment rolls are housed in two locations in Phoenix. The Arizona State Department of Library and Archives Annex had microfilmed copies of the assessments from about 1900 to 1912, while the County Treasurer's Office retains the assessments from 1930 to the present. Records for the intervening years have been lost through fire. In examining these records, I had originally

hoped to reconstruct a picture of the farming economy of the corridor area. The results were disappointing. In the early set of assessment rolls, livestock, land, and some farm equipment are itemized and taxed, but these listings give little indication of specific cropping regimes. For the more recent rolls, the only categorized listings are real estate, improvements, and personal property. Neither set of rolls describes the nature of physical improvements on these properties.

Data from the 1900 roll (Table 2.2) for William Christy, William Isaac, and Nancy Johnson, presumably a relative of the original homesteader John E. Johnson, offer little

TABLE 2.2

**Selected County Tax Assessments for Areas in the I-10 Corridor, 1900**

|  | William Christy T1N R2E Section 1 NE¼ | William Isaac T2N R2E Section 35 E½ E½ SW¼ | Nancy Johnson T1N R2E Section 1 W½ NE¼ NW¼ |
|---|---|---|---|
| Total Acres | 158 | 40 | 20 |
| Value of Land | $1040 (?) | $1100 | $880 |
| Work horses | 4 $120 | 1 $25 | — |
| Stock horses | 2 $30 | — | 2 $20 |
| Milk cows | 6 $150 | 8 $200 | 2 $50 |
| Bulls | — | — | 1 $20 |
| Stock cattle | — | — | 5 $50 |
| Calves | — | — | 5 $25 |
| Piano | $50 | — | — |
| Watch | $25 | — | — |

\* less 2 acres

more than hints about the household economies of these early settlers. Moreover, there is a marked inconsistency in the stated land values of Christy and Isaac, which most likely reflects an error of transcription on the rolls, not real differences in value. The relatively modest stock holdings on these three properties mask an intense struggle for control of water in the Salt River Valley around the turn of the century.

## Legal Decisions Over Water Allocation

Legal decisions proved to be an unexpected source of useful information for reconstructing land-use patterns in and near the I-10 corridor (Fig. 2.10). Judge Joseph H. Kibbey, an associate justice of the Supreme Court of Arizona, presided over the first bitter water battle in the valley, the momentous case of *Wormser et al.* vs. *the Salt River Valley Canal Company* in 1892 (see Davis 1897 for text of this case). The historical reasons for the suit have been summarized by Judge Kibbey:

> The earlier efforts of the settlers under these older ditches toward cultivation was confined to the production of hay and grain, and a few garden vegetables, the cultivation of which was confined to that period of the year when the water in the river was very abundant. As the settlement became older and its population increased, a more extended cultivation began to be undertaken. Instead of confining themselves to hay and grain, as above mentioned, the ranchers gradually began the planting and cultivation of alfalfa, fruits and vines, which required water during the entire year. Under the conditions as they originally existed, and as is usual in such cases, there were many usurpations and concessions of rights to the diversion of water, unnoticed at the time, or, if noticed, tacitly and without objection acquiesced in because of the then abundance of water. As the population increased and with it the more extended form of cultivation, a deficiency in water began to be noticed. While the river during the months in which hay and grain and the ordinary agricultural crops are being grown had in it a vast volume of water, this volume diminished with the advance of the season, from thousands of cubic feet per second to about, at a minimum of, three hundred cubic feet per second, and as both the increase of population and the different products to which the land was cultivated increased, the demand for water in the summer months, when the supply is the least, aggravated by an unnecessary and very considerable waste of water, exceeded the supply. This deficiency of supply made at once the question of priority of right to appropriate water, important, and that question is the subject matter of this suit (quoted in Kent Decree 1910: 6)

Kibbey responded to the issue of water allocation with his "doctrine of prior appropriation." The doctrine defined water rights for the arid and semiarid West: the farmer who is first to put water to beneficial use on his land has a prior claim to adequate water relative to all later claimants, and this water belongs to the land, not to the canal companies to distribute any way they choose (Wagoner 1970: 421).

In the years following this decision, Kibbey's orders were largely ignored. Canal companies proceeded to distribute water as they pleased, not as dictated by the courts. Judge Edward Kent, writing a subsequent decision in 1910, reviews the fate of the Kibbey order:

> Whatever may have been the legal effect of the decree entered in the Wormser suit, there was not effective attempt to enforce it or to distribute water according to its terms. Even prior to its rendition an agreement was entered into by the various canal companies whereby the parcels of land as found by such decree to be entitled to water lying under the Tempe and San Francisco canals should receive water for their irrigation to be diverted from the river by the Tempe canal according to the dates of the reclamation thereof, and in the amount of sixty-four miners' inches to the quarter section measured at the head of the canal. The balance of the normal flow of water in the river at its various stages was divided among the various canal companies in accordance with the terms of the agreement entered into by them independent of the various dates of reclamation of the land lying under the canals as such dates were found in the Wormser decree. Since such agreement the water in the river at its various stages up to 60,000 miners' inches has been distributed theoretically under the provisions of this decree, but practically and actually under the agreement entered into by the canal companies as just stated.

> To this agreement and to this distribution of the water protest has been made from time to time since the rendition of the Wormser decree, by individual land owners not content with the action of the canal company serving them with water in that regard, and various suits have been instituted from time to time in this Court to test the validity of such distribution of the water under such arrangement, none of which suits have ever come to final judgment, and of which, [one], at least, is still pending awaiting the determination of this proceeding. (Kent Decree 1910: 6-7).

Patrick T. Hurley was one such discontented valley farmer, and he initiated a suit in 1905. United States District Judge Kent presided over the famous case. Kent viewed the suit as an effort to

> . . .obtain a judicial determination and definition of the rights of the various parcels of land. . . to the use of water flowing in the Salt and Verde rivers. For a complete and effective adjudication of such rights it is necessary not only to determine the date of appropriation of water to each parcel of land, but also the amount of the water appropriated and the relative right of each parcel to the other (Judge Kent, quoted in Peplow 1979: 109).

Testimony in the suit was gathered between 1905 and 1910. Judge Kent was eventually satisfied that he had obtained reasonably accurate information regarding the first date of cultivation for 4800 landowners in the valley, and on the continuity of cultivation for these plots from 1869 to 1909. In his decree, Kent evaluates this testimony:

> A great amount of testimony has been taken as to the dates of application of water to the various subdivisions of land lying under the canals, and the results obtained have been checked in such ways as were possible. The results showing the years in which each piece of land was brought into cultivation have been tabulated, and it is believed are as accurate as is practically possible in a history which covers so great a period of time and so great an acreage. In each instance where a land owner has brought into cultivation in a given year a portion only of a section or subdivision of a section of land owned by him, but with the intention of speedily reclaiming the balance, and he or his successors in interest subsequently and within a reasonable time have brought the balance of such land into cultivation by irrigation, and such cultivation has been kept up, I have under the doctrine of relation fixed as the date of the appropriation for the whole tract the date of the first cultivation of the part.

Testimony has also in each instance been given as to the duration of cultivation. While in the main correct and accurate, it is my belief that in a number of instances the facts to the duration and extent of the cultivation of the land have been exaggerated. So far as possible the testimony given has been compared with other reliable data and in a few of such instances the testimony given has been disregarded as undoubted error (Kent Decree 1910: 7, 8).

Based upon these data, Judge Kent ordered the enforcement of Kibbey's doctrine of prior appropriation. The earliest cultivated lands were to receive first rights to the normal flow of the river, followed by the owners of lands cultivated in subsequent years. With some reservations (see Davis 1897: 53, for a discussion of the tendencies to exaggerate the extent and continuity of cultivation in the Salt River Valley by early homesteaders), these data can be used to reconstruct the early history of irrigation within the I-10 corridor (see Table 2.3). All the lands in the six sections in and adjacent to the corridor were brought into cultivation by 1881 and were continuously farmed until 1909. In future allocations of water, then, these lands were in good standing for the appropriation of water. The value of these lands for farming was thus assured.

TABLE 2.3

**Cultivation Dates**

| Township, Range | Quarter-Section | | | |
|---|---|---|---|---|
| | NE¼ | NW¼ | SW¼ | SE¼ |
| T1N R2E | | | | |
| Section 1 | 1887 | 1879 | 1879 | 1870 |
| Section 2 | 1877 | 1876 | 1876 | 1880 |
| Section 3 | 1878 | 1878 | 1878 | 1878 |
| T2N R2E | | | | |
| Section 34 | 1890 | 1881 | 1881 | 1879 |
| Section 35 | 1880 | 1880 | 1878 | 1878 |
| Section 36 | 1881 | 1880 | 1880 | 1879 |

## Salt River Project Documents

The Kibbey and Kent decrees laid the legal foundations for water rights in the Salt River Valley. In turn, the managerial structure for delivering these water allocations to farmers around Phoenix grew out of the old Salt River Valley Water Users' Association (Fowler 1904). The complex history and functioning of the association has been carefully researched and reported in several works, notably Smith (1972) and Hughes (1971). In this history of expansion in the valley, the Salt River Project (SRP) came to

incorporate into one network most of the early canal systems. I had expected that the SRP archives would contain valuable information on irrigation regimes under these old canals. This did not turn out to be the case. The Project historian provided dates for canal and lateral building but could uncover no records of cropping systems and water use in the area of the I-10 corridor, irrigated by the old Maricopa Canal. Evidently, whatever financial and technical records that were kept by these independent nineteenth century companies were lost or forgotten in an interlude of U. S. government ownership of these systems, from the passage of the National Reclamation Act in 1902 until 1917, when the Reclamation Service turned the canals over to the Salt River Valley Water Users' Association (see Smith 1972: 16, for a summary of these events).

## Booster Literature

As the canals and cultivated acreage in the Salt River Valley expanded in the nineteenth century, so did the volume of booster literature extolling the virtues of climate and fertility along the floodplain. William Christy's Arizona Improvement Company took a lead in promoting Phoenix and undoubtedly derived financial benefit from the resulting influx of settlers. Other organizations in the area did their share: the Phoenix Chamber of Commerce, the Maricopa County Immigration Union, and the *Phoenix Daily Herald* all published literature around the turn of the century. These numerous pamphlets, available in the Special Collections Division of the University of Arizona Library, revealed no specific information on historical structures within the I-10 corridor, but nonetheless offer a glimpse of the climate of optimism that early settlers such as Christy and his neighbors must have enjoyed.

The Maricopa County Immigration Union published an intelligent survey of rising land values in 1887 in a pamphlet entitled *What the Salt River offers to the Immigrant, Capitalist, and Invalid* (1887: 31-32):

Within the past year prices of land and water have rapidly appreciated in the valley, and the completion of the branch railroad has given an added impetus to the upward tendency. Many of the farms adjoining the city of Phoenix have been cut up into additions and are being sold in lots and small tracts, bringing at the rate of from $400 to $1,000 per acre. These additions are mainly intended for residences and suburban homes and all are finding a ready sale. Land from two to four miles from the city commands from $40 to $100 per acre; beyond this, lands equally as good as those mentioned can be bought at from $20 to $30 per acre. These prices are for patented lands and include a water-right sufficient to raise a crop. Only a small percentage of the lands of the valley have been proved up and paid for, the only title which four-fifths of the occupants can show being merely a possessory one.

Relinquishment claims can be secured at merely nominal figures, ranging from $2 to $5 per acre; this, of course, does not include a water-right. After securing one of these relinquishments the land must again be entered, and the new claimant is compelled to comply with the rules and regulations of the land department before he can secure final title. All the desirable land in the valley, upon which water can be brought, has been located, mainly under the Desert Act. But many of those who made such locations, being unable to comply with the rules of the Land Office and bring water upon the land within a given time, are relinquishing their rights to others. As showing the rapid increase in the value of lands near Phoenix, it may be mentioned that those tracts which are now selling at $500 per acre, could be bought three years ago for $25 and $40 per acre. Although some of these figures may appear high to the Eastern man, it must be remembered that they are very modest compared with those asked in Southern California. In that region no lands can be touched at less than $100 per acre and from that upward, while here lands capable of as varied a production, and far more fertile, can be had at from $10 to $15 per acre, including abundance of water for irrigation. To the man of moderate means these figures are far more emphatic than words, and show the advantages for settlement and investment which this valley possesses over much boomed Southern California.

The *Phoenix Daily Herald* office matched the Immigration Union in eloquence, distributing a booklet purporting to give "Reliable information on the Splendid Opportunities" awaiting settlers in Maricopa County (1886). The information, if not entirely reliable, was no doubt encouraging to prospective farmers. On the matter of canal laterals or service ditches, the *Herald* reported (1886: 18):

> These are a matter of as much importance as the canals themselves, those generally of but slight cost and quite within the limits of individual effort. If the ground has not yet been cleared, three or four men are sent ahead, who, ordinarily remove the sage brush sufficiently for a team to pass through, nearly as rapidly as a plow will follow; four or six horses are hitched to a sort of wedge-shaped scraper, or "go devil," which follows the plow, crowding the soft, broken soil out farther than the plow can do, and forming a "border." Usually about two trips of the plow and scraper, in each direction, are sufficient; small irregularities being cut down by the pick and shovel, and larger ones dug out by the use of a road scraper. Eight men with such an outfit as above described, will build from five to seven miles of service ditch per day in this soft, level soil that prevails throughout the greater portion of the valleys, at a cost of $5 and upward, per mile, the great regularity of the surface making this one of the cheapest countries to irrigate, now known. These service ditches are carried to and around the higher sides of the section of land to be irrigated, and occasionally through the land, over the surface, as in flooding grain, or through furrows along rows of trees, vegetables, vines, etc. The original flow of water is controlled by a headgate on the bank of

> the canal and by smaller headgates or merely by removing and replacing the borders of the ditches, by means of a shovel, at convenient points on the land to be irrigated.

One such ditch was built southward from the Maricopa Canal some time in the 1870s, bringing water to the lands in the I-10 corridor.

## City Maps and Aerial Photos

Maps and aerial photos confirm the general history of agricultural land use in the highway corridor, but are of somewhat limited research value. Until 1959, the corridor lay outside the boundaries of the City of Phoenix, and thus never received the precise mapping accorded to residential and commercial zones within the city (for areas within the city, see the detailed Sanborn map series, Arizona State Department of Library and Archives). Seldom are actual structures plotted on the maps covering the I-10 corridor, nor is the detail on aerial photos fine enough to interpret precisely. On the 1913 topographic maps of the Phoenix quadrangle (U.S.G.S. Phoenix Quadrangle, 15 minute series, June, 1914 edition), for example, the house on Mound 8, known to have been constructed in the 1880s and razed by fire in 1956, is not plotted. The information on this map was taken largely from a more detailed 1903 map of the Salt River Valley, compiled by the United States Geological Survey Reclamation Service (Fig. 2.11). Several structures in and near the I-10 corridor do appear on this earlier map. The Mound 8 house is plotted, along with two houses in the east half of the northwest quarter, Section 1, T1N R2E. The southern house, with an adjacent well, is outside the corridor, and presumably was destroyed in the expansion of Greenwood Cemetery. The northern house, also with a nearby well, appears to have been located within the corridor, but no traces have been discovered through previous surface surveys. Assuming that it was placed relatively accurately on the 1903 map, this house may have belonged to Nancy Johnson, who is listed on the 1900 tax assessment rolls as living on the W½ NE¼ NW¼ of Section 1 (see Table 2.2). Also shown on this map are the lateral networks running off the main irrigation canals. Several such ditches from the Maricopa Canal cross through the I-10 corridor and correspond roughly to some of the field boundaries shown in subsequent aerial photographs.

A series of city maps produced and distributed by the Lightning Delivery Company add little new information. The 1915 map (Fig. 2.12), which goes no further west than the east half of Section 1, T1N R2E, shows the S½ E¼ already planned for residential subdivision. By this date, as well, the land immediately to the west of Christy Acres had been turned into a cemetery still in existence today. In the northeast portion of the section, Christy Park had been laid out on land acquired from the descendants of Col. William

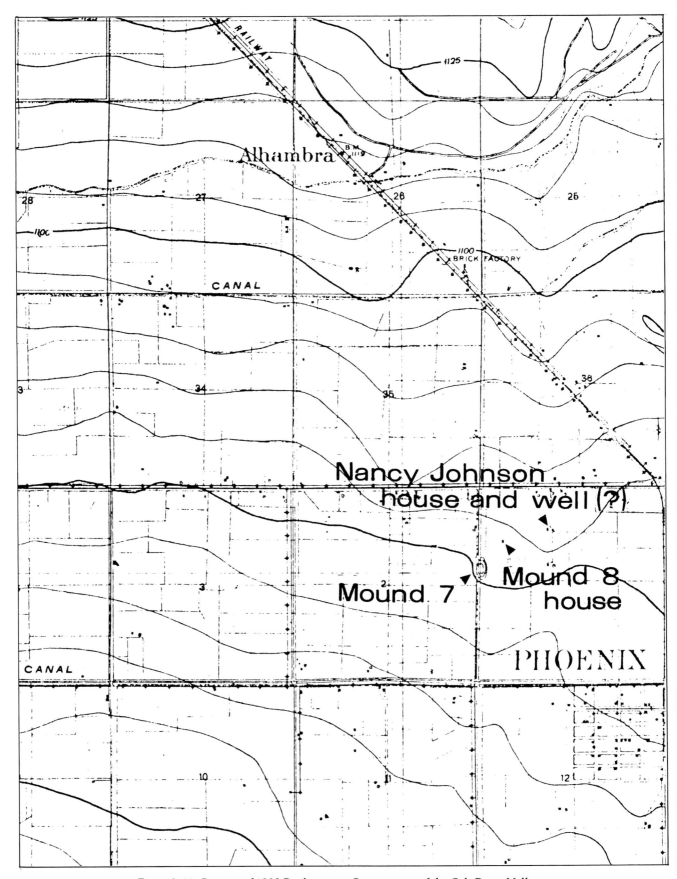

*Figure 2.11.* Portion of 1903 Reclamation Service map of the Salt River Valley.

Christy. On the succeeding maps of 1924, 1931, and 1943 (Figs. 2.13, 2.14, and 2.15), few additional alterations have occurred. Indeed, well into the 1960s farming remained the dominant land use in the corridor, a small pocket of cultivated fields in the midst of expanding commercial, industrial, and residential zones.

## Technical Reports

The final body of documentary material examined in the search for historic properties within the corridor included the numerous technical reports of the United States Geological Survey and the University of Arizona Agricultural Experiment Station (McClatchie 1901, 1902; Means 1902; Collins 1918; Matlock and Clark 1934; Davis 1897, 1903; Lee 1905; Elliot and others 1919). Like the abundant booster literature, these reports contain few specific references to properties in or near the actual corridor. But they record a vast amount of useful and largely untapped historical information on the growth of agriculture in the Salt River Valley. Diligent use of the easily-available U.S.G.S. Water-supply and Irrigation Papers and the Bulletins of the Experiment Station would provide archaeologists and historians with a firm understanding of the technical, climatic, and hydrologic parameters of large-scale irrigation systems and crops.

The short-lived Station No. 2 of the University of Arizona was, in fact, located on land once within the immediate vicinity of the prehistoric Las Colinas complex. Founded in 1890, it encompassed 80 acres along Grand Avenue, 2½ miles northwest of downtown Phoenix. This would most likely place the farm in Section 36, T2N R2E. From the start, though, the station experienced trouble. The Annual Report of the Board of Regents in 1894 noted that, "Much of this tract lies low and is not well drained, thus giving rise to an excess of alkali" (Comstock 1894: 36).

University President Theo. B. Comstock hoped to make the best of this situation and indeed felt that the research farm would eventually turn a profit:

> The accessibility of the Phoenix tract with the North and South road completed to Phoenix, and the need of experiments in reclamation of alkali lands, with the prospect that eventually the value of this area will be materially enhanced by the growth of the city, have decided me to recommend its continuance (Comstock 1894: 37).

The outcome of the University's speculative efforts is not recorded in subsequent reports. In its early years, though, the station experimented actively with a variety of crops on its own plots and on selected fields throughout the valley. Col. William Christy was a participant in one such experiment. The results are reported in the bulletin "Sugar Beet Experiments During 1898," which contains the sole piece of specific cultivation information I obtained for lands in or near the I-10 corridor (McClatchie and Forbes 1899: 194).

> Plat 5, on Col. Wm. Christy's ranch, two miles northwest of Phoenix: Soil a clayey loam, previous crop alfalfa that had been nearly killed out by pasturing. Irrigated February 16th; plowed and harrowed February 23rd; seeded February 24th. Injured by some fowls March 8th to 20th; thinned April 5th and 6th; irrigated April 6th; hoed April 11th; irrigated May 14th, when it appeared that the beets, upon account of a lack of moisture, had been injured some by the heat of the four previous days (see temperature record for year on a following page); irrigated May 26th, June 6th, and 23rd. Harvested July 26th.

William Christy's land, in fact, out-produced all the other experimental sugar beet fields in the Salt River Valley (Table 2.4).

Technical reports such as those cited above may shed light on the depositional history of the small lateral from the Maricopa Canal, near Mound 8. W. Bruce Masse, in his analysis of prehistoric canals in the area of the Hohokam Expressway, raised the possibility of using historic canal profiles, together with documentary evidence for the extent of their use, as comparisons to prehistoric canal sections (1976: 8). Useful information on water composition and irrigation cycles can be found in several of the technical reports listed above, and might be employed to supplement excavation of the small laterals in the I-10 corridor.

## Conclusions and Recommendations

Archival research on the history of the I-10 corridor uncovered little specific information on previously unknown historic features or properties. For much of its recorded history, Sections 1 and 2, T1N R2E were predominantly sparsely settled agricultural lands, irrigated by laterals from the Maricopa Canal to the north. Although little direct evidence can be marshalled on this point, these lands were probably farmed intensively. Close to the city and to developed lines of transportation, they would have been of high value and of rich potential for residential subdivision. Thus, relatively high returns on crops would undoubtedly have been necessary to allow the owners to pursue the documented use of the corridor for farming through the 1950s. The location of several historically documented houses in close association with prehistoric mounds offers some support for this assumption (see Chapter 3). The early homesteaders built precisely on the spots that would have been difficult to level and plow for crops. The historic properties that have been documented through archival research fit consistently into this landscape of intensively

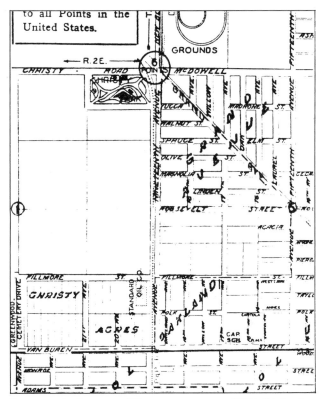

*Figure 2.12.* Section of Phoenix city map, 1915 (Lightning Delivery Company).

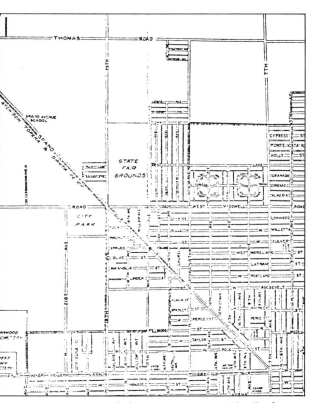

*Figure 2.14.* Section of Phoenix city map, 1931 (Lightning Delivery Company).

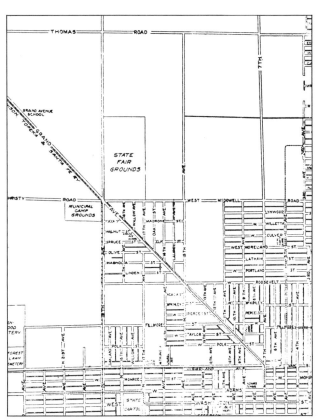

*Figure 2.13.* Section of Phoenix city map, 1924 (Lightning Delivery Company).

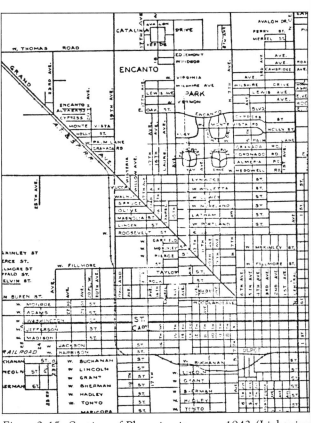

*Figure 2.15.* Section of Phoenix city map, 1943 (Lightning Delivery Company).

TABLE 2.4

**The results of William Christy's sugar beet experiment, 1898 (from McClatchie and Forbes, 1899).**

| Plat. | No. 1, Indian School. | No. 2, Canaigre ranch. | No. 3, Canaigre ranch. | No. 4, Murphy ranch. | No. 5, Christy ranch. | No. 6, Grier ranch. | No. 7, Fowler ranch. | No. 8, Fowler ranch. | No. 9, Hough ranch. | No. 10, Experiment farm |
|---|---|---|---|---|---|---|---|---|---|---|
| Previous crop | Vegetables | None | Alfalfa | Alfalfa | Pasture | Pasture | Vegetables | Vegetables | Vegetables | Pasture |
| Character of soil | Clay | Sandy loam | Clayey loam | Gravelly loam | Clayey loam | Sandy loam | Fine adobe | Fine adobe | Fine adobe | Fine adobe |
| Per cent of fine material | 86.34 | 58.37 | 76.86 | 64.97 | 86.58 | 76.42 | 98.93 | 98.93 | 94.66 | 99.72 |
| Per cent of humus | 0.904 | 0.448 | 0.807 | 0.719 | 0.876 | 0.840 | 1.13 | 1.13 | 1.53 | 1.56 |
| Maximum water capacity percentage | 37.34 | 33.55 | 41.79 | 37.36 | 40.42 | 34.69 | 51.11 | 51.11 | 49.9 | 56.62 |
| Date of seeding | Feb. 21 | Feb. 22 | Feb. 22 | Feb. 24 | Feb. 24 | Feb. 25 | Feb. 1(?) | Mar. 1 | Mar. 14 | Feb. 26 |
| Date of thinning | Mar. 29 | Apr. 12 | Apr. 2 | Mar. 31 | Apr. 5 | Apr. 6 | Apr. 14 | Apr. 13 | Apr. 15 | Apr. 12 |
| Times irrigated | 6 | 6 | 5 | 7 | 6 | 5 | 4 | 3 | 3 | 3 |
| Times cultivated | 2 | 1 | 1 | 1 | 1 | 2 | 1 | 1 | 1 | 1 |
| Times hoed | 2 | 2 | 3 | 2 | 2 | 3 | 1 | 1 | 3 | 2 |
| Date of harvesting | July 28 | July 27 | July 27 | July 22 | July 26 | July 16 | July 30 | July 30 | Aug. 2 | Aug. 3 |
| Number of beets per square rod | 188 | 201 | 182 | 161 | 184 | 116 | 175 | 171 | 168 | 138 |
| Average weight of beets | 10.1 oz. | 4.5 oz. | 15.5 oz. | 11.3 oz. | 18.0 oz. | 24 oz. | 15 oz. | 19 oz. | 11 oz. | 21.3 oz. |
| Yield of beets per acre | 10.3 tons | 4.6 tons | 13.8 tons | 9.0 tons | 16.5 tons | 15.2 tons | 13.0 tons | 16.3 tons | 14.5 tons | 15.2 tons |
| Per cent sugar in beets | 13.3 | 17.5 | 13.7 | 15.7 | 14.1 | 11.1 | 15.1 | 12.0 | 12.3 | 13.0 |
| Purity coefficient | 80.6 | 86.0 | 77.6 | 82.1 | 78.7 | 75.5 | 75.4 | 74.8 | 77.4 | 77.2 |
| Approximate yield of sugar per acre | 2085 lbs. | 1200 lbs. | 2705 lbs. | 2210 lbs. | 3395 lbs. | 2275 lbs. | 2655 lbs. | 2600 lbs. | 2525 lbs. | 2785 lbs. |

cultivated fields, canals, and dispersed residences and out-buildings.

Evidence for the possible existence of several previously undocumented historic features within the corridor segment was revealed by archival research. The house and associated well noted as possibly having been occupied by Nancy Johnson appear to have been located within the area now covered by the corridor. Because of the scale and accuracy of the 1903 map on which these features are plotted, however, it is impossible to determine precisely their former location. No traces of these features have been recorded by the several surveys of the corridor, and it may be that any remains of them have been completely destroyed or are now covered by the paved lot presently occupied by the Phoenix Fuel Company. In addition, several historic canal segments that appear to have been located in the area of the corridor are also seen on the 1903 map. One of these is in the far western end of the corridor segment under consideration, near 30th Drive, while the others lie in the eastern end of the corridor, immediately west of Interstate 17. These latter canal segments may have been associated with the still existing canal segment lying to the east of Mound 8.

With respect to the house and well, the existing information on their former location is not sufficient as a basis for a testing program. With respect to the historic canal segments, one of them may still be seen, and it may be expected that the others will be encountered during the proposed testing for prehistoric resources. Assuming these canal segments are encountered, they will be dealt with according to the guidelines for the proposed testing of prehistoric resources outlined below. The approximate location of the house and well has been noted, and the possibility that these features might also be encountered has been considered.

Thus, testing specifically focused on historic resources is not proposed. Those historic features documented may be encountered during the proposed testing for prehistoric resources, and it is possible, though unlikely, that additional undocumented historic remains might be encountered. Should any additional historic remains be encountered, the State Historic Preservation Officer will be contacted immediately and decisions regarding the appropriate treatment of such resources made at that time.

# Chapter 3

# PREHISTORIC RESOURCES

by David E. Gregory

This chapter deals with the prehistoric remains within the I-10 corridor segment under consideration and is divided into two parts. The first part deals with the results of research conducted preliminary to, and in the course of, designing the proposed field-testing program. Several basic questions generated to orient this research are presented and discussed, followed by the results of these preliminary studies. The second part deals with the research questions to be addressed during the field-testing phase of the project and discusses the methods to be employed in answering these questions.

## Preliminary Research

### Research Questions

The focus of the preliminary research has been the collection and summary of data relevant to understanding (1) the original nature and extent of the site of Las Colinas and its relationship to the proposed I-10 corridor, and (2) the various processes that have affected the site since its abandonment, with specific attention to those areas of the site within the I-10 corridor.

It is necessary at the outset to have as precise an idea as possible about what the original nature of the remains of Las Colinas may have been. The information now available from the site as well as any additional data that may be collected in the future must be understood in the context of the site as a whole. Because of the locational isomorphism between modern urban communities and the prehistoric settlements that were their predecessors, and because of the biases and limitations of archaeological research accomplished prior to the destruction of many major ruins in the Phoenix area, we have only the sketchiest data concerning the areal extent and internal structure of many of the major Classic period Hohokam sites. Because the size, distribution, and arrangement of features within prehistoric sites are primary sources of data bearing on a wide variety of

research questions, it is worthwhile to attempt the reconstruction of these attributes for Las Colinas to the degree possible. Of particular concern for the present project is the area of the site subsumed by the I-10 corridor: we wish to determine how the portion of the site included within the corridor relates to the entire site as it once existed. This has obvious and direct bearing on the formulation of a subsurface testing plan and on the interpretation of any data that may result.

The following questions may be posed:

1. *What is known of the original nature and extent of the prehistoric remains grouped together as the site of Las Colinas?*
2. *How does the original extent of Las Colinas relate to that segment of the I-10 corridor now under consideration; and what prehistoric remains have been documented within that corridor segment?*

A second major area of interest is the nature and effects of various processes that have affected Las Colinas since its abandonment. This information is important in (1) interpreting the observations of features at the site made by different individuals at different times (2) assessing the possible existence and condition of any subsurface materials (3) structuring decisions regarding the specific placement and relative frequency of trenches to be excavated during the field-testing phase of the project, and (4) interpreting the general stratigraphy and specific remains encountered during the testing. Again, the area of the site within the corridor segment is of particular concern. The following questions may be posed:

1. *What processes have affected the remains of Las Colinas since its abandonment, and how?*
2. *What processes have affected that portion of the site within the I-10 corridor, and how?*
3. *What have been the effects of similar postoccupational processes on other archaeological sites in the area?*

## The Original Nature and Extent
## of Las Colinas

In the interest of clarity and ease of reference, it is useful to begin at the end point and work back in discussing the data presented below. The results of research directed at the collection of data relevant to the determination of the former nature and extent of Las Colinas are summarized in preliminary fashion in the form of a reconstructed site map (Fig. 3.1). This map, then, serves as the point of departure for a discussion of the means by which the reconstruction was arrived at and for subsequent consideration of the individual features, materials, and relationships that have been documented.

The map shows the archaeological features that have been at one time or another described or pictured, including the major mounds at the site, the major canals, and other features and materials whose locations have been reported. To the extent possible, the size of the mounds and associated features has been adjusted to scale, and the locations given are the most precise that may be derived from the existing data. There is, of course, some variability in the accuracy of the map. The sources and nature of this variability are discussed in the text that follows and, to the degree possible, the variability has been encoded in the symbols used on the map and explained in the accompanying legend.

The pertinent segment of the I-10 corridor is shown, divided into the numbered sub-areas (1 through 6) of the corridor to be employed in this discussion. These sub-areas will be further described and illustrated below. Also shown on the map are several major streets, as well as the section and quarter section lines. For purposes of contrast and orientation, Figure 3.2 shows the locations of the major archaeological features and the I-10 corridor segment superimposed on a 1940 aerial photograph of the area.

### Sources of Data

The ruins of Las Colinas (also Casas de las Colinas) have attracted at least the passing attention of professional archaeologists and other interested observers for over a century. However, with two notable exceptions (Moorehead 1906; Hammack 1969), much of the available information on the site consists of large scale maps and brief descriptions of surface features resulting largely from observations made before 1930. Despite their brevity and incompleteness, it is indeed fortunate that these early observations were set down in one form or another, for, as we shall see, most of the major features at the site had been destroyed by that time. Thus, while we have specific information regarding at least two major features at the site, the primary source of what we may now know of the original nature and extent of Las Colinas is to be found in the collective work of several

early observers of the archaeology of the Salt River Valley. Before proceeding to employ their work for our purposes, it is useful to review the efforts of these individuals and others who have at various times concerned themselves with the site of Las Colinas.

Las Colinas probably appears on the map of the Salt River Valley prepared by the Hemenway Expedition (Haury 1945: 11). There are three sets of dots representing ruins in the vicinity of Las Colinas, but the site is not named on this map and determination of the specific mounds or other features represented by these dots is impossible.

The earliest documented dealings with the site were undertaken by Warren K. Moorehead, then Curator of Archaeology of the Phillips Academy of Andover, Massachusetts. Between November 1897 and June 1898 Moorehead conducted work at several major sites in the Salt River Valley in and around Phoenix (Moorehead 1906: 66, 89-96). One of these sites was Las Colinas, at that time called the Kalfus Ruins* (Moorehead 1906: 98). Moorehead placed several trenches in and around the feature later to be designated Mound 4, and at several other unidentified locations at the site.

Beginning a decade before Moorehead's work and continuing until at least 1903, H. R. Patrick undertook the work of recording the canal systems and ruins in the Salt River Valley. Patrick, a long-time Phoenix resident and a surveyor (Fewkes 1909), published the results of his observations in 1903 in the form of a short article and accompanying map (Patrick 1903). Las Colinas, considered by Patrick to be one of seven "of the more important of these cities" (Patrick 1903:9), is labeled as ruin 'B' on this map and is shown as having five large mounds (probably numbers 1, 3, 4, 7, and 8) and numerous smaller ruins (Fig. 3.3). The relationship of Las Colinas to the major canal systems may also be seen.

In 1908 Jesse Walter Fewkes received a grant from the Smithsonian Institution to collect comparative data to be used in conjunction with his then recently completed work at Casa Grande (Fewkes 1908, 1909). He recorded numerous ruins in the Salt-Gila Basin, as well as in the Middle Gila, San Pedro, and Santa Cruz drainages, and published the results of his excursions in the article "Prehistoric Ruins of the Gila Valley" (1909). H. R. Patrick is acknowledged by Fewkes in this article, and it may have been Patrick himself who guided Fewkes to the ruins of Las Colinas, still referred to in 1908 as the Kalfus Mounds (Fewkes 1909: 421). Included in Fewkes' article is the only known map of Mounds 3 and 4 and their associated compound wall, along with a brief discussion of these and another mound, probably Mound 7.

The present numbering of the mounds at the site, as well as the assignment of its present name, may be attributed to O. A. Turney. Turney is well known as an early observer

*The origin of this name remains obscure.

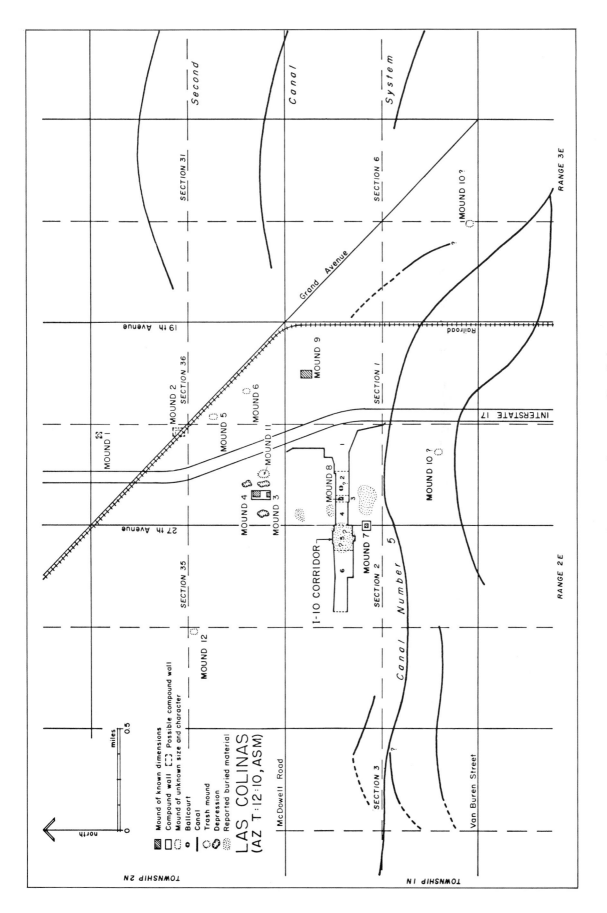

*Figure 3.1.* Reconstructed site map of Las Colinas.

*Figure 3.2.* 1940 aerial photograph of Las Colinas area, showing locations of the major mounds, several canal segments, and the I-10 corridor.

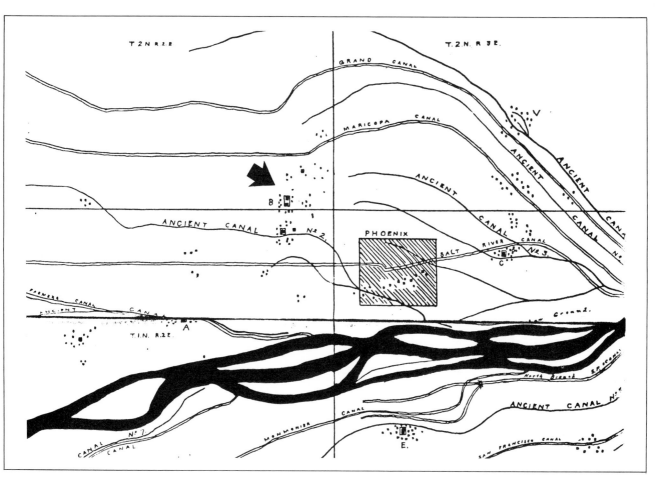

*Figure 3.3.* Portion of Patrick's 1903 map showing Las Colinas and its mounds.

and recorder of the canal systems and ruins of the Salt River Valley. On the map accompanying his 1924 publication *Land of the Stone Hoe* (Fig. 3.4), and subsequently on the map published with the more extensive *Prehistoric Irrigation in Arizona* (1929) (Fig. 3.5), Turney shows Las Colinas as having 10 numbered mounds, a ballcourt, and numerous smaller ruins. Again, the major canal systems are shown. The site and its numbered mounds are briefly discussed in the text of his second book (Turney 1929: 92-94).

With the exception of the map constructed for this report, the most complete map of the Las Colinas area proper may be found in the notes of Frank Midvale (Midvale, n.d.) (Fig. 3.6). This site map was derived largely from Turney's earlier maps but was augmented on the basis of observations by Midvale during 50 years in the area and overlapping in time with the work of Turney. Two mounds (numbers 11 and 12) are added to Turney's original 10. The final form of this map is dated June 1968 and was based in part on Midvale's recollections at that time.

In 1968 the Arizona State Museum conducted intensive investigation of the Mound 8 area. This work was directed by Laurens C. Hammack and sponsored by the Arizona Department of Transportation. The work concentrated primarily on the excavation of major portions of Mound 8, but extensive backhoe trenching was accomplished east of the mound as well. The results of Hammack's work represent the most detailed information available on any feature at Las Colinas and provide a source of data bearing on several research questions outlined above (Hammack 1969; Hammack and Sullivan 1981). This material will be referred to later in this report.

Several surveys of the proposed I-10 corridor have been conducted by the Arizona State Museum, the most recent in 1978. The results of this survey provide some additional information concerning the occurrence and relative abundance of surface materials present and represent the most recent formal data collection undertaken at the site.

Over the last two decades, and especially since the 1968 work at Mound 8, several incidental observations of archaeological materials in the vicinity of the corridor have been made. Although of limited utility, these observations do bear on the question of the nature and distribution of

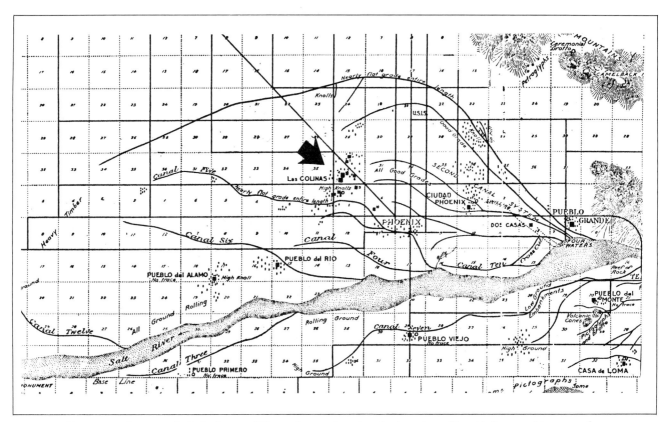

Figure 3.4. Portion of 1924 edition of Turney's map showing the location of Las Colinas and its mounds.

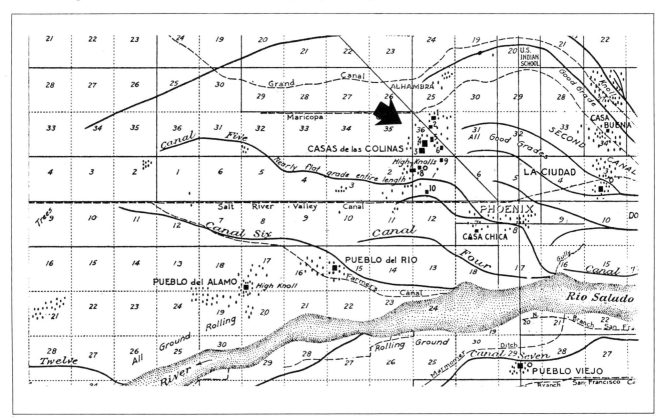

Figure 3.5. Portion of 1929 edition of Turney's map showing the location of Las Colinas and its mounds.

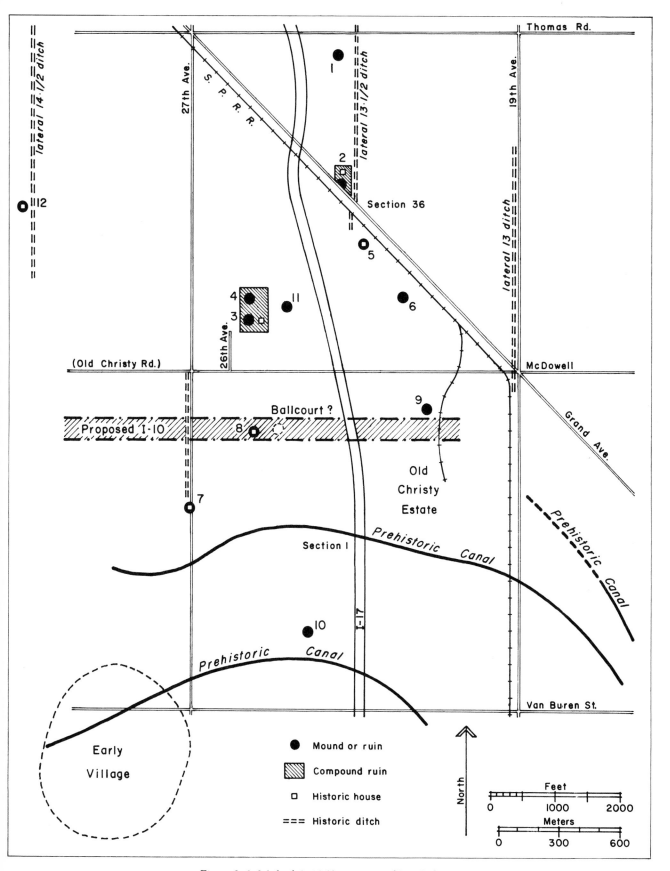

*Figure 3.6.* Midvale's 1968 site map of Las Colinas.

features and materials at the site. In addition, recent examination of aerial photographs on file at the Photogrammetry Section of the Arizona Department of Transportation has revealed the existence of several previously unrecorded canal segments in the Las Colinas area.

Before proceeding, it is prudent to enter a brief caveat concerning some of the information sources consulted. Noted above is the fact that much of what we may now know of the original nature and extent of Las Colinas depends upon observations made before 1930. Specifically, five men—Moorehead, Patrick, Fewkes, Turney, and Midvale, all now deceased—were responsible for producing most of the existing data. Since much of what follows depends on the work of these individuals, two general points of caution and perspective should be made. The first concerns the individuals themselves, the second deals with the attention they paid to Las Colinas.

Only two of these individuals—Moorehead and Fewkes—were professional archaeologists. Thus, we may have some basic expectations about their training, the kinds of variables they paid attention to, and so forth. The other three—Patrick, a surveyor; Turney, an engineer; and Midvale, one-time tour guide and jack-of-all-trades—were united not by profession but by a common and perhaps consuming avocational interest in the prehistoric remains of the area. In many cases, all we have is the say so of one of these individuals that a feature was located in a particular location, was of a particular size, and had particular attributes. Should I assume the truth of the statement that there was once a ballcourt located to the east of Mound 8, even in the absence of the remains of such a feature searched for during the 1968 excavations? Should I believe that Mound 7 was 25 feet high? Should I take for granted that Mound 2 had a compound wall around it?

In order to fully evaluate the observations of these men, it would be necessary to become as familiar as possible with their individual biographies. Just as the observations of Moorehead and Fewkes must be evaluated in terms of the state of archaeology at the time and in terms of their particular experience and demonstrated expertise, so must the observations of these other three individuals be evaluated in terms of the times in which they lived and the kinds of men they were, in terms of their biases, abilities, and beliefs. I do not pretend to have this kind of familiarity with them, and I am not entirely certain that such a psychosocial reconstruction and critique would be of great utility to the present study. However, it is certainly worthwhile to point out the problems inherent in the use of the sort of data these men have provided.

None of the five individuals, including the archaeologists, were concerned with the site of Las Colinas *in particular*. In the case of Moorehead and Fewkes, theirs was a passing interest no greater than that held for any other archaeological site. Moorehead put trenches in several sites, and there is no reason to believe that he was concerned with Las Colinas as anything more than an example of the type of ruin to be found in the area. In fact, his continuing interests were in the eastern United States, and his excursion to the American Southwest has some of the aura of a busman's holiday. The brevity of Fewkes' comments on the site is sufficient evidence to demonstrate only a passing interest. Likewise, the three avocational archaeologists were as concerned with the canal systems as with the sites themselves, wrote more about the canals than about the ruins, and do not appear to have been any more interested in Las Colinas than in any other site. Thus none of the five who left records of their early observations at Las Colinas were concerned with the site beyond its identity as a major site having perhaps more than the usual number of mounds, one site among many with which they were familiar. This undoubtedly accounts, at least in part, for the incomplete record we now have before us.

Neither of these points is intended as an indictment of these individuals. As we have already noted, without them we would have no notion of the original character of the site. The concerns are introduced simply to put the available data in proper perspective and to note that these factors must be considered in evaluating their work and what we may learn from it.

## Location and Extent of the Site

All but two of the major mounds that have been at one time or another included as part of Las Colinas lie within the 2-square-mile area defined by Section 36, T2N R2E, Section 2, T1N R2E, or the area at present bounded by Thomas Road on the north, 19th Avenue on the east, Van Buren Street on the south, and 27th Avenue on the west. The exceptions to this generalization are Mounds 10 and 12. Mound 12, added to the site map by Midvale in 1968 and about which little else is known, lies fully outside the described area in approximately the middle of Section 35, T2N R2E. Two locations for Mound 10 have been given in various sources; one, in the SW¼ of Section 6, T1N R3E, is also outside the 2-square-mile area containing most of the features. The problem of the location of Mound 10 is discussed below.

On both Patrick's map (1903) and on the various editions of the Turney map, most of the "smaller ruins" associated with the major mounds of Las Colinas are also within Sections 1 and 36 as described above. A few are shown scattered in the extreme eastern portions of Section 35, T2N R2E, and of Section 2, T1N R2E. Whether the dots representing these smaller ruins are simply generalized symbols or were intended to represent particular ruins in particular locations is unclear, and little additional information is available concerning the exact nature and locations of these "smaller ruins." For this reason, these ruins have been excluded from the site map (Fig. 3.1). An "early village" is shown on Midvale's map in the SE corner of Section 2, T1N R2E and in the NE corner of Section 11, T1N R2E (see Fig. 3.6). No additional information is available concerning this early site.

On the basis of the early maps of the site, it would appear that the primary axis of feature density may be best represented by a line running from the southwest corner of Section 1, T1N R2E to the midpoint of the section line separating Sections 25 and 36, T2N R2E. The midpoint of this axis falls approximately at Mounds 3 and 4, placing these features roughly in the center of the site, as suggested by Moorehead (1906: 98). Some crude estimate of the original size of the site may be obtained by simply measuring the area inside a line connecting the outermost major mounds. The area thus included is approximately 1.3 square miles or 850 acres. If a similar line is drawn and the area covered by the mounds *and* the smaller ruins at the site is included, the figures are approximately 1.9 square miles or 1200 acres, roughly a 40 percent increase. The Section 1 location for Mound 10 has been used in these calculations rather than the Section 6 placement because of the questions concerning the location of that mound and in the interest of producing a conservative estimate.

Other sites in the general area which appear to have been partly contemporaneous with Las Colinas include Pueblo del Rio, situated some 2.5 miles to the southwest; Casa Chica, lying just over 2 miles southeast; and La Ciudad, 3 miles east (Fig. 3.5).

With respect to the major canal systems, all major features and most minor ones at Las Colina lie north of the long Canal Number 5, or Canal Colinas (Turney 1929), and were located some 3 miles west of its head and approximately 3 to 5 miles north of the Salt River. The site was situated immediately west of the ends of three branches of the Second Canal System, while another branch of that same system terminated approximately 1 mile due north of Mound 1 in Section 25, T2N R2E. The large northernmost canal of the Second Canal System passed "above" the site some 2 miles north. Thus the major canals in the area formed an arc or "U" opening to the west around the site (Turney 1929; see Fig. 3.5).

The position of Las Colinas relative to these canals is quite interesting, in the sense that the inhabitants of this large site would have benefited from the water provided by these canals without being in direct physical control of the headgates. The position of Las Colinas with respect to the major canal systems on the north side of the Salt River is thus structurally similar to that of the large site of Los Muertos on the south side of the river (Haury 1945). While it is not possible here to follow up on these preliminary observations, the examination of the overall relationships between site size and distribution and location on the major canal systems may prove a fruitful avenue of inquiry bearing on Classic period Hohokam social and political organization. For the present, it may be noted that, in addition to

its size, the position of Las Colinas relative to the major canal systems that surrounded it may be a significant indicator of its former importance (see Wilcox 1979).

At first glance the topographic situation in which Las Colinas was located would appear to be simple. The land in the area rises slowly as one moves north from the Salt River at a rate of only 25 feet approximately every 2 miles. The contour just south of Mound 7 and near the southern extent of the site is 1075 feet, while the contour just north of Mound 1 and on the northern edge of the site is 1100 feet. There are no major topographic features in the general area, therefore, it would seem that Las Colinas was situated on the gradually sloping expanse of land constituting the ancient floodplain of the Salt River. While this description is not inaccurate, closer examination reveals the possibility that the topographic location of the site was more subtle and complex than cursory inspection would indicate; the topography and the geologic history may explain in part (1) the roughly linear distribution of features at the site, and (2) the reason for the termination of several major segments of the Second Canal System immediately east and north of the site.

Turney noted that the ruins of Las Colinas were "placed along a slight rise of ground which protected them from water" (1929: 92). This slight rise may be seen faintly in the contour lines of the area and appears to extend both north and south of the site. Figure 3.7 shows the site in relation to the contours of the area as they were mapped in 1902-1903 (Lee 1904; Harper and others 1926; see also Fig. 2.11). The location of the rise as indicated by the topographic contours corresponds well with the distribution of major features at the site. It may be that the magnitude of variations in the natural topography had already been reduced somewhat by plowing and leveling of the land, and that the ridge on which Las Colinas was located may have been a more apparent feature at one time.

Also shown in Figure 3.7 is a rough reconstruction of the drainage patterns that once existed in the area of the site. This reconstruction is based on the 1902-1903 contours, water table contours from the same period, and soil distribution maps (Lee 1905; Harper and others 1926). While this map represents only an approximation of former patterns, several interesting points may be noted.

It is likely that the drainage pattern illustrated followed the ancient channel of Cave Creek, originating in the Phoenix Mountains to the north. Even during the prehistoric occupation of Las Colinas, Cave Creek would not have been a fully channelized wash. Rather, runoff from the north would have been broadly localized in the area of the filled-in channel of an even more ancient, probably Pleistocene, drainage. Prior to the modification of the area by modern occupation and during the occupation of Las Colinas, Cave Creek would have been a wide, shallow, braided wash, more narrow in some places than in others. It appears that this wash would have drained around the low ridge on

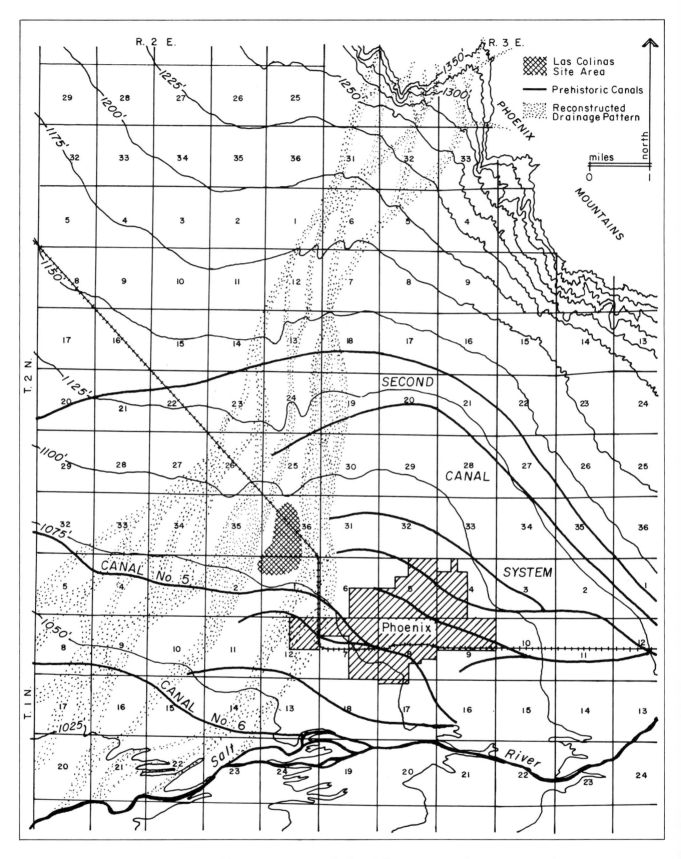

*Figure 3.7.* Reconstruction of drainage patterns in the Las Colinas site area, showing topographic contours as of 1902–1903 (based on Lee 1905).

which Las Colinas was situated on both the east and west sides. In times of above-normal runoff, then, the site would indeed have been protected from flooding.

Noted above is the fact that four major segments of the Second Canal System terminate east and north of the site. As may be easily seen in Figure 3.7, the termination points of these canals correspond approximately to the eastern side of the broad Cave Creek drainage area. It may have been that the ridge on which Las Colinas was situated, in combination with the presence of the Cave Creek drainage running along it on either side, would have presented a significant barrier to the westward extension of these canal segments. To skirt this ridge, the canals would have had to dip considerably to the south before continuing west. This, in turn, would have put major portions of them in the area of the drainage, a situation which could precipitate frequent damage, repair and other mechanical problems as well.

While the analysis presented here is rudimentary, it does suggest that the location of Las Colinas and to some extent its aerial boundaries were determined by topography and drainage patterns. Further, the termination of several canal segments in the area of the site may also be partially explained by these factors.

## The Nature of the Mounds

It has long been recognized that one of the distinguishing charateristics of Hohokam sites is the presence of artificial mounds (Haury 1976). It is also known that these mounds vary considerably in their particular morphological characteristics—in their size and shape, and in the manner in which they were originally constructed—and that they were functionally and temporally variable as well. For purposes of understanding the nature of Las Colinas, both in terms of its specific characteristics and by way of providing a basis for comparison with other sites, it is necessary to have some idea of the character of the mounds once present there. Further, since the mounds of Las Colinas are undoubtedly the most fully recorded features at the site, they are a logical starting point for a consideration of the nature of the site as a whole. The available information concerning each of the numbered mounds at Las Colinas is summarized and discussed below, followed by a consideration of the other known features and materials documented as being part of Las Colinas.

### Mound 1

Little is known of Mound 1. It may be that the northernmost of the five "temples" shown on Patrick's map (1903) represents this mound, as the location shown corresponds approximately to that shown later for Mound 1 by Turney and Midvale. Because of the scale and accuracy of the maps, however, the mound shown on Patrick's map could possibly be Mound 2. By 1929, Mound 1 had been graded down and was at that time in use as a base for a haystack yard (Turney 1929: 92). Midvale gives the dimensions of Mound 1 as being 125 feet by 125 feet horizontally and 9 feet high (ASU site files), and he suggests that it had a compound. If such a compound were present, a Classic period date is likely. Figure 3.8 shows the approximate location of the mound as it appeared in the 1930s, while Figure 3.9 shows the location as it appeared in 1973.

### Mound 2

As with Mound 1, information concerning Mound 2 is scarce. Turney notes that by 1929 the mound had been removed and that all that remained was a slight rise on which a house had been built (Turney 1929: 92). Figure 3.10 shows this house as it appeared in 1973, and Figure 3.11 shows the same house as it appeared during the late 1940s or early 1950s. Turney does note that "much interesting material" (1929: 92) was discovered when irrigation ditches near the mound were dug, but this tells us nothing of the original character of the mound. Midvale's map shows the mound as being surrounded by a compound wall, but there is no further substantiation for the existence of this feature. If there was such a compound, then it is likely that the mound represented the remains of a ruined houseblock, a platform mound, or both, and that it dated at least in part to the Classic period.

### Mounds 3 and 4

Aside from Mound 8, the best documented features at Las Colinas are Mounds 3 and 4. Since both mounds were situated within the same large compound wall, they will be discussed together.

Although the report is brief and includes no maps, Moorehead's discussion of his work at Mound 4 provides information concerning the size of the compound wall and of the two mounds, the nature of construction of Mound 4, and the nature of several associated features (1906: 98-103). Additional observations and a map by Fewkes (1909), plus Turney's and Midvale's materials, are other sources of information on these features.

The compound wall surrounding Mounds 3 and 4 must have been impressive. Moorehead gives the dimensions of the wall as being 160 m north-south and 80 m east-west (1906: 98), or approximately 525 feet by 262 feet, and states that the wall was 3 m wide and stood 0.5 m high at the time of his work there. The horizontal dimensions are corroborated through observations made by Fewkes some 10 years later. He gave the measurements in feet, and described the compound as being 500 feet north-south by 260

*Figure 3.8.* Photograph showing location of Mound 1 as it appeared in the late 1930s.

*Figure 3.9.* Photograph showing location of Mound 1 as it appeared in 1973.

*Figure 3.10.* Photograph showing location of Mound 2 as it appeared in 1973.

*Figure 3.11* Photograph showing location of Mound 2 as it appeared sometime in the late 1940s or early 1950s.

feet east-west (1909: 421). Fewkes' map of the compound and the associated mounds is reproduced in Figure 3.12. Note that the north-south measurement shown on the map is 520 feet, at variance with the 500 feet given in the text; however, the 520 feet on the map is closer to the measurement given by Moorehead, and the east-west dimensions given by both individuals are in close agreement. It is of some interest that by the time Turney observed the two mounds the compound wall could be fully traced only on the north and west sides (1929: 93) and does not appear on any of his maps.

It is clear from Moorehead's descriptions that Mound 3 was the higher of the two, and that he excavated only in Mound 4:

> The two larger buildings. . . are both surrounded by an adobe wall. . . . To the south, this wall forms a sort of platform extension of the *south or highest temple* . . . .*The higher temple to the south* may present more interesting structure, but *it was thought best not to attempt its exploration* (1906: 98, 103; emphasis added).

Moorehead gives the outside dimensions of Mound 4 as "fifty meters east-west and 78 meters north-south" (1906: 98), but hedges his bets, suggesting that

> Archaeologists might differ as to where the wash or accumulation at the base end and the natural surface begins, hence these measurements might be a meter

more or less upon each side and end. The writer would suppose that the original building was something like 35 x 60 meters (Moorehead 1906: 98).

Of course the latter measurement allows for something more than "a meter more or less," but some basic idea of the size of the mound may be gained.

Regarding the height of Mound 4, Moorehead notes the presence of depressions or "reservoirs" to the east and west of the compound, and states:

> Above these low places, the ruin stands four and one-half meters. From the level, the height is about thirty-three meters [sic], but the ends are lower by one half or two thirds m. than the central positions (1906: 98)

Clearly the "thirty-three meters" is an error, and it would appear that he meant three and a third or 3.3 m. A figure of slightly more than 3 m agrees well with the following description of the trench cut through the central portion of Mound 4:

> *When the main trench was about three meters down* we observed numerous pottery fragments, ashes, charcoal, and broken bones. These were in little pockets or ash pits, ranging from half a bushel to as much as three or four bushels. One large ash pit was three feet in depth. No floors could be traced and *no walls were found in the central cut save at the ends.* We cleaned out the central cut to the original base, exposing six meters by nineteen meters, and found little or nothing. It was even difficult to find the original base. No general floor

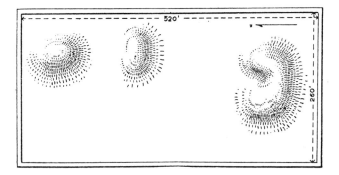

*Figure 3.12.* Fewkes' map of compound containing Mounds 3 and 4.

seemed to have existed, and we abandoned the central part of the cut completely mystified as to the purpose of the ruin at this point (1906: 102; emphasis added).

This passage suggests that Mound 4 was indeed a platform mound, one that had been built over borrow pits filled with trash (such as those discovered at Mound 8), cremation pits, or both. Moorehead's discussion also indicates that there were rooms on top of the mound (1906: 102-103; see also Schroeder 1953: 176-177). Since Mound 3 was higher than Mound 4, it is quite likely that it, too, was a platform mound. The general impression one gets of these two mounds and their associated compound wall recalls Compound B and associated structures at Casa Grande (Fewkes 1912), and also perhaps some similarity to the main mound at Mesa Grande (Moorehead 1906: 63).

Turney's discussion of Mounds 3 and 4 introduces some confusion regarding the relative size of the mounds. He states the following:

> No. 3, partially destroyed, is 105 feet east and west and 105 feet wide and stands 14 feet high; apparently it was oriented. It stands 130 feet south of No. 4.
> No. 4 was worked on by Prof. W. K. Moorehead in 1897; it measured 180 feet east and west and 150 feet wide and stood 30 feet high with its outer walls 30 inches thick (1929: 92-93).

The horizontal dimensions given here for Mound 4 would have the feature considerably smaller in at least one dimension than was documented by Moorehead, and would have the mound larger in the east-west dimension than the north-south, the reverse of the situation indicated by Moorehead. Turney's measurements also make Mound 4 taller than Mound 3, again the reverse of what was observed by Moorehead. Several things may account for these discrepancies.

It is likely that Mound 4 was already partially destroyed by the time Turney observed it, since Fewkes noted in 1909 that both these mounds were "rapidly being destroyed" (1909: 421). This could account for the differences in the horizontal dimensions given by the two men. With respect to the 30-foot height given for Mound 4, this simply seems

anomalous, since Moorehead repeatedly noted that the southernmost mound was the highest. It is also possible that Turney was not only incorrect about the 30 feet, but that he also reversed the heights of the two mounds in his writing. The 14-foot height for Mound 3 is relatively consistent with Moorehead's descriptions, as it would make Mound 3 some 1 m to 2 m higher than Mound 4.

Turney also notes the presence of the depressions described by Moorehead and gives measurements for them as well as for an associated trash mound:

> To the northeast 250 feet was a borrow pit three hundred feet square and three feet deep, while to the southeast was another 300 feet north and south and 150 feet wide and four feet deep. To the east of this latter was a midden mound parallel with it and covering an equal area (1929: 93).

This midden was probably the feature later designated as Mound 11 by Midvale (see below).

The type of architecture represented, as well as a sherd of Jeddito Black-on-yellow reported from the midden by Turney (1929: 92), would indicate a Classic period date for Mounds 3 and 4. It is possible that an earlier occupation was present, however, given the trash from the base of Mound 4 described by Moorehead.

Figure 3.13 shows Mound 3 as it appeared sometime during the 1920s, while Figure 3.14 shows the approximate former location of Mounds 3 and 4 as it appeared in 1973.

*Mound 5*

Mound 5, which was graded down and which had a house built on its remnant prior to 1929, is now completely gone (Turney 1929: 93). Figure 3.15 shows the approximate former location of the mound as it appeared in the 1930s, while Figure 3.16 shows the same location in 1973. Plowing in the area of Mound 5 was still turning up artifacts in the late 1920s (Turney 1929: 93). No information concerning the characteristics of Mound 5 is available, and its chronological position is unknown as well.

*Mound 6*

Mound 6 had entirely disappeared by 1929 and no other information exists concerning this feature. Figure 3.17 shows the approximate former location of the mound as it appeared in 1973.

*Mound 7*

In 1929 Turney described Mound 7 as follows:

> No. 7 can be seen dimly; the county paved road [now 27th Avenue] passed through its middle and a house is on its eastern slope. We remember when this ruin

*Figure 3.13.* Mound 3 as it appeared sometime during the 1920s.

*Figure 3.14.* Approximate location of Mounds 3 and 4 as it appeared in 1973.

West of Phoenix there are two large mounds that may be called Kalfus Mounds, both of which, *especially the smaller,* are being rapidly destroyed. *A road has cut through one of these* and the material is being rapidly carted away for use elsewhere. . .*the smaller of the compounds measures 275 by 210 feet* (1909: 421; emphasis added).

As noted above, the larger of the two compounds refer-red to by Fewkes was that containing Mounds 3 and 4. The smaller would appear to be Mound 7. First, Mound 7 appears on Patrick's map as having a compound wall, and Fewkes was well aware of Patrick's work and dealt directly with him (Fewkes 1909: 419). Fewkes notes:

> The best published map we have of the distribution of aboriginal ruins and irrigation ditches in this region is by Mr. Patrick, of Phoenix, Arizona. . . . (Fewkes 1909: 419).

Second, the only other major mound with a road through it at that time would have been Mound 2, cut by Grand Avenue. Mound 2 is probably not shown as a major feature on Patrick's map, and in any case is not shown as having a compound wall. Finally, the horizontal dimensions given by Turney (1929) agree fairly well with those given by Fewkes for the "smaller compound."

From the dimensions given by the various observers and the probability that Mound 7 was enclosed by a compound, it would appear that the mound represented the remains of a platform mound, probably with associated roomblocks. Thus, a Classic period date is suggested.

With the exception of Mound 8, Mound 7 appears to be the best preserved of any of the major features at Las Co-linas. The remnant eastern slope of the mound may be easily seen today (Fig. 3.19), and recent examination of the area

stood 25 feet high and from the top of the eroded walls the orientation was clear; it was 250 feet east and west and 180 feet wide (1929: 93).

The house mentioned by Turney as well as the road cutting through it may be seen in the photograph, Figure 3.18, taken during the 1920s. The mound and the house may be seen on the 1903 map of the area made by the Reclamation Service (see Fig. 2.11). The mound is shown as being over 15 feet high at the time.

Mound 7 is pictured by Patrick (1903) as having a com-pound wall. Substantiation for the existence of this feature comes from Fewkes, as does information concerning the condition of the mound in 1908.

*Figure 3.15.* Approximate location of Mound 5 as it appeared in the early 1930s.

*Figure 3.16.* Approximate location of Mound 5 as it appeared in 1973.

*Figure 3.17.* Approximate location of Mound 6 as it appeared in 1973.

*Figure 3.18.* Photograph of Mound 7 prior to 1929 showing the road that is now 27th Avenue cutting through it.

*Figure 3.19.* Mount 7 as it appears today.

*Figure 3.20.* Area immediately northeast of Mound 7, showing outlines of adobe walls.

immediately to the north and east of this feature revealed the existence of wall alignments (Fig. 3.20). One of these walls may represent a portion of the former compound wall, while others clearly define the remains of former rooms or individual structures. Abundant surface material may be found on and around the remaining portions of Mound 7, and the presence of red wares would support the Classic period date suggested by the architecture. It has also been reported that buried materials are to be found over a large area east of Mound 7.

## Mound 8

The 1968 excavations at Mound 8 produced one of the most complete and detailed bodies of information available concerning a Classic period platform mound (Hammack 1969; Hammack and Sullivan 1981). The site map resulting from this work is reproduced in Figure 3.21 and an aerial photograph of the excavations in progress may be seen in Figure 3.22. While it is impossible to detail all the features represented on this map and to discuss the entire

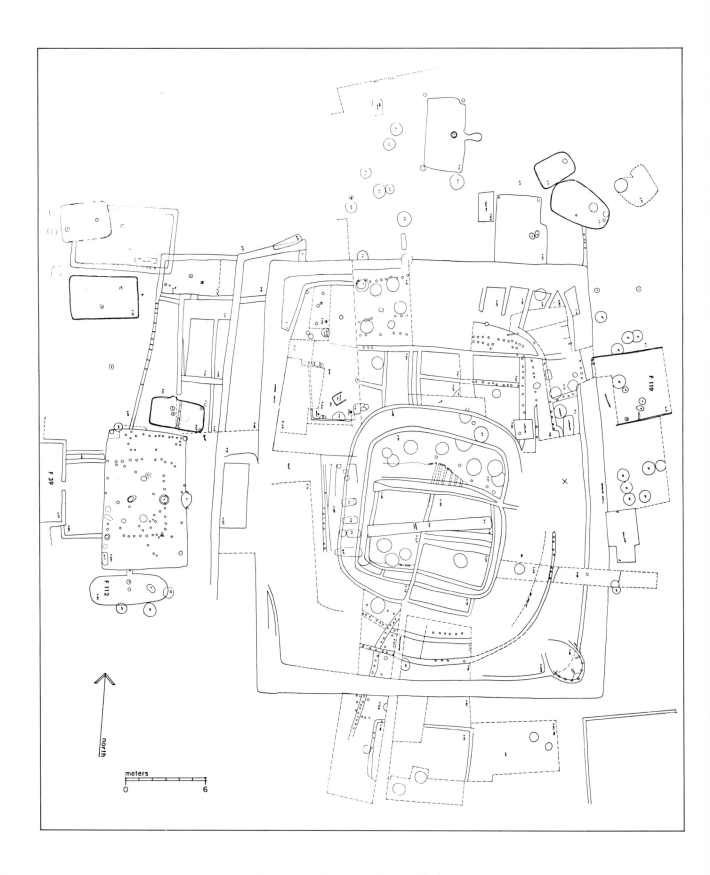

*Figure 3.21.* Site map of Mound 8 area.

*Figure 3.22.* Aerial photograph taken during 1968 excavations at Mound 8.

body of materials recovered from the site, the map provides a basis for a summary of the relevant aspects of what is known of Mound 8. Some basic idea of the size and complexity of the mound may be gained and compared to what is known of the other mounds at the site. The features specifically referred to here and in following sections are labeled on the map.

In the 1880s an adobe house was constructed on top of the mound, and remained until 1956, when it burned. The lengthy occupation of this dwelling insured the survival of Mound 8, despite substantial disturbance to the surface and interior of the mound created by the unusual basement of this house and by the construction of other structures associated with the dwelling. Figures 3.23 and 3.24 show the house as it appeared in 1917 and in the late 1940s or early 1950s, respectively.

The excavations revealed that the mound was in its earliest recognizable form in the shape of a square with rounded corners, and it was constructed of trash and earth-filled cells formed by an interlocking series of post-reinforced adobe walls. The mound witnessed at least four stages of expansion, each employing a similar type of construction and each resulting in a slightly larger and higher feature. Each construction stage was culminated by the capping of the mound with a layer of adobe.

*Figure 3.23.* Mound 8 as it appeared in 1917, looking east-northeast.

During the penultimate construction stage, a massive adobe wall was erected enclosing the series of earlier mounds and changing the shape of the mound to a full rectangle with squared corners. This feature may be easily seen on the map in Figure 3.21. The dimensions of the mound at the completion of this wall and its associated vertical extension would have been approximately 27.5 m

*Figure 3.24.* Mound 8 as it appeared in the late 1940s or early 1950s, looking east-southeast.

north-south, 23 m east-west, and slightly over 2 m high. These measurements agree fairly well with those presented for the mound by Turney, who had the mound 115 feet north-south, 80 feet east-west, and 10 feet high (1929: 94). The final construction accomplished was the extension of the mound to the west by means of a wall attached to that side of the massive adobe wall.

The only feature partially preserved on the former surface of the mound was part of an adobe-walled structure, located on the northwest portion of the feature. An archaeomagnetic data of A. D. 1297 to 1373 was obtained from a sample taken from this structure. Associated with the area immediately around the mound, however, were numerous structures, including both pit houses and coursed caliche constructions, sometimes superimposed over one another and thereby providing evidence of their relative temporal positions.

The ceramic materials recovered from the interior cells of the mound and the 14 archaeomagnetic dates obtained from samples taken during the excavations provide conclusive evidence that the construction and sequential modifications of the mound and associated features occurred almost entirely within the Classic period. All but one of the archaeomagnetic dates came from features around the mound rather than in or on it (range A.D. 1155 to 1467).

There is some evidence for an earlier occupation in the area of the mound. The remnant of a post-reinforced wall was found on the south side of the mound and extending beneath the walls of the earliest construction, and a Sacaton type pit house (Feature 112) was located west of the mound. There was also abundant Sacaton trash in the retaining cells of the earliest construction stage, and even a few sherds of Colonial and Pioneer material. However, this earlier material was inevitably accompanied by equally abundant Classic period ceramics (red wares, Casa Grande Red-on-buff), indicating that the earlier trash had probably been acquired elsewhere for use as fill in the mound.

Sixteen inhumations and six cremations were recovered during the excavations. All the inhumations were in or immediately adjacent to the mound itself, while the cremations were discovered through backhoe trenching just southeast of the mound. It is interesting that this distribution of inhumations in mounds or roomblocks and cremations outside of those features and to the east occurred consistently at Los Muertos and may be seen at other sites (Haury 1945, 1976).

An interesting matter concerning Mound 8 is the apparent lack of a compound wall surrounding the feature. No trace of such a wall was recognized during the 1968 excavations. If the mound did not have a compound around it, it would be the only known example of a Classic period platform mound lacking such a feature. There is some evidence to suggest that a wall did exist, and there are reasons why it would not have been discovered.

On the western side of the mound, Feature 39 was mapped as having short wall segments attached to and extending from its north and south sides (see Fig. 3.21). Since this feature was not entirely excavated, and since the extent of the excavation was isomorphic with the approximate alignment of these wall segments, the ultimate length and alignment of the wall represented is unknown. It may be that Feature 39 represents a structure built into the compound wall, much in the manner of several structures in groups II, XIII, XVII, and XXI at Los Muertos (Haury 1945). Further, immediately to the west and slightly south of Feature 39, a possible north-south wall alignment may be seen today by the anomalous distribution of vegetation. It is also possible that this alignment represents part of a compound wall, perhaps an extension of the southern wall segment associated with Feature 39. Thus, the western limits of the 1968 excavations would have prevented the discovery of a compound wall segment on this side of the mound. Why was the wall not seen in other areas of the excavation?

On the north side, the extent of the excavations could have easily been *within* the compound wall. On the south side the same is true, and in any case only limited trenching was done south of the mound. On the east side, the plowed area reached quite close to the mound, and it may be that the compound wall had been completely removed here. It is possible, then, that Mound 8 did have a compound wall, and there are reasons why it may not have been discovered during the 1968 excavation. This will be an important question to resolve in future dealings with the site.

Mound 8 represents the only well-documented example of the in situ developmental sequence of a Classic period platform mound. Further, it is one of the few instances where broad areas around a mound have been exposed, and where, therefore, we have good data regarding the sequential use of space around a mound. Published materials dealing with the 1968 excavations at Mound 8 consist of a preliminary report (Hammack 1969) and a full report (Hammack and Sullivan 1981) published by the Arizona State Museum. In addition, the author is currently engaged in further studies of the implications of Mound 8 materials for an understanding of Classic period Hohokam social and political organization.

The information gained from Mound 8 is important to several topics relating to the proposed testing outlined below. The pertinent data will be referred to in the appropriate sections of the discussions that follow.

## Mound 9

Mound 9 met its demise in 1884, when it was graded down in the course of building the home of Col. William Christy (see Chapter 2). Turney notes that the mound was once 200 feet east-west, 300 feet north-south, and 5 feet high. The configuration presented by these measurements suggests that the mound may have been the remains of a large compound and/or roomblock rather than a platform mound or trash mound. If this is the case, a Classic period date is indicated. There were also apparently several borrow pits associated with this feature, the largest of which "was so deep that it was surrounded with palms and used as a carp pond" (Turney 1929: 94). The presence of borrow pits also argues for the identity of the mound as an architectural feature rather than as a trash mound. "Many stone articles" (Turney 1929) were discovered when Mound 9 was graded.

## Mound 10

We know perhaps less of Mound 10 than any others. There is no information on the original nature of the feature, and even its approximate former location is problematic. On Turney's 1924 map, Mound 10 appears in the southwest quarter of Section 6, T1N R3E, nearly a mile from the nearest major mound of Las Colinas, Mound 9. In the text of the 1929 book, Mound 10 is also described as being in this location: "just north of Van Buren Street and west of Fifteenth Avenue" (Turney 1929: 94). The map accompanying this text, however, places the mound in the southwest quarter of Section 1, T1N R2E. This placement is duplicated on Midvale's later map. Since the position of Mound 10 within Section 1 is essentially similar to that shown earlier and described within Section 6, it would appear that a simple error was made when the 1929 edition of the map was drafted, and that this error was later perpetuated by Midvale.

The picture becomes more complicated, however. When photographing the former locations of the mounds in 1973,

*Figure 3.25.* Location in Section 1 within Greenwood Cemetery, showing rise thought to be the remains of Mound 10 as it appeared in 1973.

Hammack searched in Section 1 for the location shown on Turney's 1929 map and on Midvale's later map. This location was then and is now within the Greenwood Cemetery. Figure 3.25 shows the photograph taken at that time in Section 1: a definite rise may be seen, thought at the time to represent the remains of Mound 10. In addition, Bruce Huckell observed prehistoric sherd and lithic materials in a cleared area immediately east of the location shown. The grass covering the mound obscured any artifacts which, if present, could have provided some definite clue as to the nature of this feature.

Two basic explanations may be suggested, neither completely satisfactory. First, it is possible that Mound 10 *was* located in Section 6, in the position described by Turney and shown on the 1924 map, and that the 1929 map represents an error later repeated by Midvale. Thus, the feature photographed in 1973 is either not prehistoric or it represents the remnants of a prehistoric feature never given a number. If this is the case, then we must ask the question: Why was Mound 10 included as a part of Las Colinas rather than as part of Casa Chica, a site much closer to the mound than any of the other features at Las Colinas?

Second, and possibly less likely, it may be that both the 1924 map and Turney's 1929 description were in error, that Mound 10 was, in fact, in Section 1, and that the 1973 photograph shows the remains of Mound 10. This explanation, however, flies in the face of the fact that Turney states that Mound 10 had disappeared by 1888. If a remnant of the mound still existed, why did Turney not note this fact as he did with some other mounds?

In any case, we know nothing of the original character of Mound 10, and the vagaries of working with the early maps and descriptions of these ruins are clearly illustrated.

### Mound 11

Mound 11 is one of two mounds added to Turney's original map of the site by Midvale. He located it immediately east of the large compound containing Mounds 3 and 4, and some clue as to the nature of Mound 11 comes from Moorehead's description of the area around these two large mounds:

> To the east, lying between it [the large compound] and *a smaller ruin,* is a low place, evidently a reservoir, also from whence earth was taken for the adobes (1906: 98; emphasis added).

The location would also fit Turney's description of a large trash mound associated with Mounds 3 and 4 (1929: 98) and situated to the east of these features. The size of the mound given by Turney (150 feet by 300 feet) would indicate quite a substantial feature. Mound 11 is therefore identified as this feature and is shown as a trash mound on the site map in Figure 3.1 in the location given by Turney and Moorehead. As noted above, a sherd of Jeddito Black-on-yellow was reported as having come from this feature, indicating a Classic period date. The relationship of this mound to the large compound containing Mounds 3 and 4 is similar to that seen between trash mounds and several of the groups at Los Muertos (Haury 1945).

### Mound 12

Other than the fact that it appears on Midvale's map as having a house on it, nothing is known of Mound 12. It is possible that one of the smaller ruins pictured on the maps of Patrick and Turney represents this mound, but specific identification is impossible.

## Other Features and Materials

While it is undoubtedly the case that the mounds were only the most obvious features at the site, and that a variety of other features existed, we have only the most minimal information concerning these less impressive remains. As has been pointed out, the presence of numerous features besides the major mounds is indicated by the "smaller ruins" pictured on maps of Patrick and Turney, while the statements of both Turney and Moorehead suggest that both trash mounds and ruined roomblocks were present at the site:

> After completing work upon the larger ruin [Mound 4] we examined a number of small ones in the same group. In these we found no walls save in the case of one. There was a well defined room, the floor being a meter below the present surface . . . . The other ruins seemed to be more the nature of mounds resulting from long living upon one spot, or due to the accumulation of debris (Moorehead 1906: 102).

As already noted, both Moorehead and Turney state that large depressions, probably borrow pits and possibly reservoirs, were associated with the large compound containing Mounds 3 and 4 (Moorehead 1906: 98; Turney 1929: 92) and with Mound 9 (Turney 1929: 94). Incidental observations provide some additional data concerning the nature and distribution of features and materials other than the major mounds.

Excavations were conducted in 1968 by Arizona State University at an Arizona Public Service substation immediately south of McDowell Road and east of 27th Avenue, less than a quarter mile northwest of Mound 8 (ASU site files). At least one buried pit house and several inhumations were recovered in this area. The ceramics recovered indicate an early Classic period occupation, roughly contemporaneous with the initial construction stages of Mound 8. The remains of an unusual burial were also salvaged from the vicinity of Mounds 3 and 4 by Arizona State University in 1961 (Morris and El-Najjar 1971). During the excavation of structural foundations north of corridor Sub-area 4, immediately north and west of Mound 8, at least one and possibly more buried house floors were observed by Laurens C. Hammack. Although the date of these house floors is not known, they were buried at least a meter below the ground surface that existed prior to the excavations.

Recent discussions with maintenance personnel from the Greenwood Cemetery indicate that buried materials are consistently encountered in the course of digging graves in the northern part of that cemetery. From the descriptions given, it would appear that cremations, trash pits, and probably other features are present. The distribution of these features, marked on a cemetery map by Raul Cordova of the maintenance staff, indicates an almost continuous distribution of materials east of Mound 7 for approximately a quarter mile (see Fig. 3.1).

There are secondhand reports that buried materials were encountered during the laying of sewer lines along 27th Avenue in the corridor area, according to Hammack. Nothing is known of the nature of these remains, but the presence of such buried materials would be consistent with the density of surface materials now to be seen in corridor Sub-area 5 immediately to the west and with the proximity of the area to both Mounds 7 and 8.

## Relationship of the Site
## to the I-10 Corridor

### General Spatial Relationships

If we assume the general north-south axis of feature density described above for Las Colinas, the I-10 corridor crosses that axis at a roughly perpendicular angle, approximately one-half mile south of the center of the site as represented by Mounds 3 and 4. Mound 8, of course, is included in the corridor and is located in the approximate center of the corridor segment under consideration. The ballcourt pictured to the east of Mound 8 on Turney's maps would appear to have been within the area now defined by the corridor, as would at least one of the dots representing a smaller ruin (see Figs. 3.4 and 3.5), just west of 27th Avenue. Mound 7 lies less than a quarter mile south of the corridor along 27th Avenue, and buried materials of unknown character have been reported from areas to the north and south of the corridor, and in the corridor along 27th Avenue (see Fig. 3.1).

### Documented Remains from
### Within the Corridor

The existing information concerning archaeological materials located specifically within the I-10 corridor comes from (1) the 1968 excavations at Mound 8 (2) materials recorded during the 1978 survey of the corridor, and (3) incidental observations. Known archaeological materials from each corridor sub-segment are reviewed below. Since Sub-area 3 (Mound 8) has already been treated, it will not be included here. The locations of the sub-areas discussed may be seen in Figure 3.1.

*Area 1*

None of the early maps of the site area shows any features in the vicinity of Area 1. On Midvale's map of Las Colinas, a canal segment running off the major Canal Number 5 to the north is pictured in the western half of Section 6, T1N R3E (see Fig. 3.6). The portion of this canal nearest the corridor is shown as a dotted line. If the trajectory of this canal is projected, and if it is assumed that the canal may have been longer than pictured by Midvale, it is *possible* that the canal could have cut through the southern portion of Area 1. However, if the inferences outlined above concerning the ridge on which Las Colinas was situated and the relationship of that ridge to the ancient wash channel lying to the east are correct, it is unlikely that this was the case.

Five short backhoe trenches were placed in the western end of Area 1 during the 1968 excavations at Mound 8 (see page 67). These trenches were not systematic in their placement and produced no cultural materials or evidence of subsurface features.

During the 1978 survey of the corridor, nine sherds, ten flakes and two cores were observed in Area 1, scattered over the area and in no apparent concentration.

Thus, aside from the few artifacts observed during the 1978 survey, and the remote possibility that a canal segment may have once cut through the area, there is absolutely no evidence to suggest the presence of subsurface materials or features in Area 1.

*Area 2*

Twenty-nine backhoe trenches of varying lengths and alignments were excavated in Area 2 during the 1968 excavations at Mound 8 (see Fig. 3.22). A single trash pit was uncovered some 30 m due east of Mound 8, and six cremations were found an equal distance from, and slightly southeast of, the mound. In the remainder of the trenches, no cultural materials or features were found, which seems as surprising now as it did to Laurens Hammack, archaeologist in charge at the time.

It is obvious that the 1968 trenches covered a considerable area, and the failure of most of these trenches to encounter any remains provides some idea of the distribution of subsurface materials in the area. The only portion of Area 2 not substantially tested during 1968 was the southeast corner. It may be concluded, therefore, that while some subsurface materials may certainly exist, the relative density of materials in Area 2 is low.

The initial impetus for the trenching of the area in 1968 was the ballcourt reported by Turney to have been located immediately east of Mound 8. No indication of the former presence of this feature was detected, however. As will be discussed, it is quite possible that this feature was entirely destroyed by plowing, and if such a feature was once located in Area 2, the absence of other types of features and deposits may be less surprising than it would initially appear. While the actual function of ballcourts is still debated by some, there is general agreement on the special nature of these features. In those cases where data exist, the density of features around ballcourts appears to be low (Haury 1976; Fewkes 1908).

*Area 3*

Area 3 contains Mound 8, which has been discussed in some detail above. The area exposed during the 1968 excavations may be seen on the map and aerial photograph in Figures 3.21 and 3.22.

## Area 4

Undoubtedly some surface remains exist in Area 4, since one of the houses discovered during the 1968 excavations extended into the very eastern edge of this area and was not completely excavated because of this (Feature 39; see Fig. 3.21). In addition, a slight rise may be observed in this area today running almost the entire length of the eastern end. This rise represents at least some subsurface features. In March 1980, examination of the area revealed a north-south alignment devoid of grass, a typical indicator of buried caliche walls. As noted above, if there was a compound wall at Mound 8, it is likely that some remnant of it exists in the eastern end of Area 4.

How far the remains associated with Mound 8 may extend to the west in Area 4 is unknown, since we have no information concerning archaeological materials in the remainder of the area. Scattered sherds and flakes may be found, but the overall density is low. Observations of buried houses immediately north of this area, and the abundance of surface materials found immediately west of Area 4 in Area 5, are both factors suggesting the possibility that other buried materials exist.

## Area 5

During the 1978 survey of the corridor, abundant surface materials were noted in Area 5. This material has been brought up by the excavation of shallow trenches around the lots of houses which once occupied most of the area and which have now been removed, and thus actually originated below the ground surface. These trenches are distributed over the entire area, with the exception of the northeast corner. The presence of abundant artifacts in Area 5 lends some substance to the reports of buried materials encountered during the excavation of sewer trenches along 27th Avenue immediately to the east. Gravel cover obscures the ground surface over most of the area, and other than in and near the trenches, only an occasional artifact may be seen.

On the 1924 and 1929 editions of Turney's map, one dot representing a smaller ruin is shown in a location that would be in or very near Area 5. The materials that may now be observed in the shallow trenches in the area may thus represent the remains of the feature or features represented by Turney, perhaps a trash mound or houseblock.

## Area 6

During the 1978 survey, 8 to 10 sherds, four flakes, two cores and a single mano fragment were observed scattered over this large area. No apparent concentrations were present. Since one of the ditches in Area 5 is located on the boundary between the two areas, it is possible that whatever remains are represented by the materials in those trenches extend over into Area 6. As noted, one of the dots on Turney's map would indicate the presence of some sort of feature in the general area.

## Summary

The segment of the I-10 corridor under consideration appears for the most part to be within the overall boundaries of Las Colinas derived from the early maps of the site. The corridor passes over one major mound (Mound 8), and just north of another (Mound 7). Buried archaeological materials have been reported both north and south of the corridor, as well as within the corridor in the area of 27th Avenue.

Existing data suggest that archaeological materials specifically within the corridor are concentrated in and to the west of Area 3, which includes Mound 8, or in Areas 3, 4, and 5. Area 2 contains subsurface features, but the overall density appears to be low. No substantial evidence exists that would indicate the presence of subsurface materials in Area 1, and except for its extreme eastern portions, this is true of Area 6 as well. Table 3.1 summarizes the overall probabilities of the existence of subsurface remains in each corridor sub-area, based on existing data.

TABLE 3.1

**Probability of Subsurface Archaeological Remains in the I-10 Corridor**

| Corridor Sub-area | Probability of Subsurface Remains Based on Existing Data |
|---|---|
| 1 | Low |
| 2 | Certain (low density) |
| 3 | Certain (Mound 8) |
| 4 | Certain (at least in eastern end of area; no evidence for rest of area) |
| 5 | Certain (nature of remains unknown) |
| 6 | Low (except in extreme eastern portions of area) |

## *Postoccupational Processes Affecting Las Colinas*

In order to provide as complete a picture as possible of the processes to which Las Colinas has been subjected and to document the known or expected results of the action of those processes, three basic topics are addressed below. First, a general history of postoccupational processes within the Las Colinas area is presented, and the effects on known features at the site discussed. Second, the corridor area is treated specifically with respect to the nature and effects of postoccupational processes. Finally, some attention is given to the effects of similar processes at other sites in the area.

## General History and Effects

Little may be said of the site from the time of its abandonment until 1868, when the sectioning survey was accomplished. Nonetheless, we may surmise that whatever deterioration the ruins may have experienced during this 400-year period was primarily the result of natural processes rather than those effected by humans. This situation changed radically and rapidly with initial Anglo occupation and the expansion of settlement in the Phoenix area.

The sectioning survey was barely completed when large blocks of land in the vicinity of Las Colinas were initially cultivated. Table 3.2 gives the beginning dates for cultivation of land within the 4-square-mile area that subsumes Las Colinas that was under continuous cultivation in 1909.

TABLE 3.2

**Starting Dates for Cultivation of Parcels Recorded under Continuous Cultivation as of 1909**

| Township, Range | Section | Portion of Section | Cultivation Starting Date |
|---|---|---|---|
| T2N R2E | 35 | S½ | 1878 |
| | | N½ | 1880 |
| | 36 | SE¼ | 1879 |
| | | W½ | 1880 |
| | | NE¼ | 1881 |
| T1N R2E | 1 | SE¼ | 1870 |
| | | NE¼ | 1877 |
| | | SW¼ | 1878 |
| | | NW¼* | 1879 |
| | 2 | W½ of SE¼ | 1876 |
| | | SW¼ | 1876 |
| | | N½* | 1877 |
| | | E½ of SE¼ | 1880 |

* indicates parcels that include portions of the I-10 corridor

While the parcels of land listed may in some cases have included houses and associated domestic space, the dates provide an excellent picture of the rapid and widespread conversion of the desert into farmland that occurred in the last 20 years of the nineteenth century.

The primary use of the land in the Las Colinas area for agriculture continued well into the present century. The map and series of aerial photographs (Figs. 3.26, 3.27, 3.28 and 3.29) illustrate the appearance of the area in 1913, 1936, 1940, and 1963. Although cultivated fields are not shown, it is clear from the 1913 map that the area was at that time on the northwestern periphery of Phoenix and that few houses and roads were present. The canal running roughly north-south through Sections 36 and 1 attests to the agricultural character of the area in 1913. While residential areas had expanded somewhat, cultivated fields still dominated the area in 1936 and 1940 (Figs. 3.28 and 3.29). In the immediate vicinity of Mound 8 cultivation continued into the late 1950s (Figs. 3.30 and 3.31). By 1963 much of the area was no longer under cultivation, but even at that late date several active fields were present. There were also large, open areas in 1963, especially in the NE¼ of Section 2 and W½ of Section 1; the remnants of plow furrows in these areas may be easily seen in the photograph of Figure 3.29. Large open fields are present even today, and there is one sizeable cultivated field fronting on 27th Avenue northeast of Mound 8.

The degree to which archaeological features in cultivated areas are able to resist the plow and maintain their original integrity or at least some recognizable configuration undoubtedly depends on a variety of factors—among them, the original nature and depth of the feature, postoccupational rates of deposition before plowing, the frequency and duration of plowing, the type of plow used and the kinds of crops grown, the extent to which leveling of the land is employed, and perhaps even the perseverance of the plowman. In the case of Las Colinas, we know that in several isolated instances documented above, such features as pit houses, inhumations, cremations, and trash pits have survived the plow and remained buried and intact. On the other hand, the 1968 excavations at Mound 8 provided evidence that one portion of an adobe-walled structure had been completely destroyed by plowing, and that several cremations and a trash area had been at least partially disturbed or destroyed. It is possible that the ballcourt reported to be east of Mound 8 was entirely removed by plowing. Data regarding the effects of cultivation in the Mound 8 area and at other sites in the area are discussed in further detail below.

In terms of the Las Colinas area as a whole, it may be logically assumed that minor surface features and shallow buried remains would have been substantially disturbed in the course of plowing and leveling of the land for cultivation. Very early—that is, by the first decade of the twentieth century—such features as small roomblocks, trash mounds, cremations, and other features of similar magnitude would have been disturbed, displaced, and ultimately destroyed. Many of the "smaller ruins" shown on the Patrick and Turney maps and an unknown number of less obtrusive archaeological features may have met their demise as a direct result of cultivation.

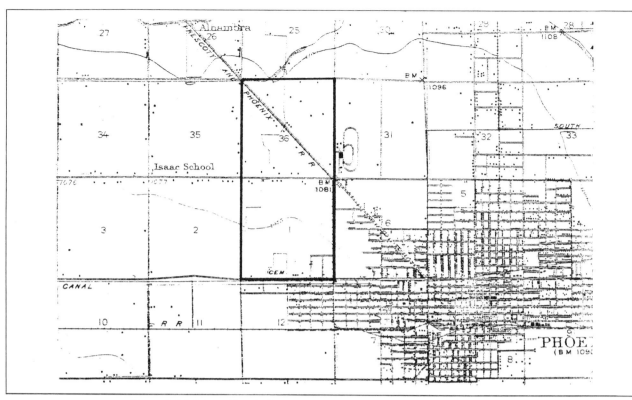

*Figure 3.26.* Map of Las Colinas area in 1913, showing roads and residences.

*Figure 3.27.* Aerial photograph of Las Colinas area taken in 1936.

*Figure 3.28.* Aerial photograph of Las Colinas area taken in 1940.

As was the case in prehistoric times, the modern use of the area for agricultural purposes depended upon canal irrigation. In addition to actual plowing of the land, the construction of modern canals would have disturbed any prehistoric features in their paths. Mound 7 was cut through not only by a road (see Fig. 3.18) but by the Lateral 14 canal as well; Turney noted in 1929 that the excavation of irrigation ditches in the area of Mound 2 was still bringing up artifacts.

While we may not, for the most part, document the specific effects, it may be stated with some confidence that cultivation of the land and the associated construction of canals were early and probably significant processes affecting some of the remains of Las Colinas.

Although the numbered mounds at the site do not appear to have been directly affected by plowing, two activities related to the development of the area's agricultural potential had the most significant effects on the "high knolls": the building of houses and the construction of roads.

It is probably the case that the larger mounds at Las Colinas were spared from the plow simply because they were too big to be easily plowed over, and ultimately, under. Instead, it seems that the mounds provided convenient and perhaps even preferred locations for the construction of houses, barns, and other architectural features. It may also be that the mounds held the additional advantage of not tying up tillable land in domestic space. Some four hundred years after their abandonment, then, at least several of the mounds resumed what may have been in part their original function: artificial eminences upon which dwellings and other structures were constructed.

Six of the 12 numbered mounds at the site had houses constructed either directly on top or on their sides sometime between 1880 and 1929. One of the remaining six was leveled and used as a base for a haystack yard, in some ways a similar function. In the case of Mound 8, it is certain that the construction of a house on the mound at an early date insured its survival. Although much of the surface of the

*Figure 3.29.* Aerial photograph of Las Colinas area taken in 1963.

mound and some portions of its interior were severely disturbed by the house and its unusual basement, the fact that so much of the mound was discovered intact in 1968 may be directly attributed to the lengthy occupation of the house on its summit. Houses constructed on other mounds had far less sanguine effects, as in the case of Mound 9, which was entirely graded down in 1884 when Col. Christy's house was built on it (Turney 1929: 93). The construction of houses thus had variable effects on the mounds of Las Colinas, in at least one case preserving the feature, in another resulting in total destruction. Road construction, however, was decidedly destructive to the mounds.

Early in the settlement of any area, roads must be built, and the area then northwest of Phoenix was no exception. The construction of roads later to become the major and minor thoroughfares of metropolitan Phoenix had severe effects on the mounds in two ways. First, the mounds were

directly affected by having roads cut through them; and second, they were indirectly affected because they constituted a localized and convenient source of quality fill for road beds.

Even prior to the initial cultivation of the Las Colinas area, and before the sectioning survey was accomplished, the supply road from Fort McDowell to Wickenburg crossed the site, passing either between or very near Mounds 3 and 4. By 1908 the road later to become 27th Avenue had cut through Mound 7 (Fewkes 1909: 421; Fig. 3.18), and by 1913 Grand Avenue had intersected Mound 2. Although most of the mounds were not in the direct paths of major roads or streets, the adobe construction employed by the original builders of the mounds proved instrumental in their ultimate destruction, as noted by Fewkes: "This 'caliche' is much sought after by Americans, as it makes a very firm road bed" (1909: 421). The bulk of Mounds 3, 4, and 7 was

*Figure 3.30.* Photograph of Mound 8 taken during the late 1940s or early 1950s.

*Figure 3.31.* Photograph of Mound 8 taken sometime after 1956, when the house burned.

removed and used for this purpose, and severe damage to these mounds, especially Mound 7, had already been incurred by the time Fewkes observed them in 1908 (Fewkes 1909). The remaining portions of Mound 4 were completely removed by dirt haulers in 1927, and Mound 3 suffered a similar fate some four years later (Turney 1929: 92; *Arizona Republic* article dated February 23, 1931; this article includes a picture of Mound 3 being hauled away). Thus the use of material from the mounds for road fill had begun by at least the first decade of the present century and, in the case of Mounds 3 and 4, this process had resulted in their complete obliteration by 1931. Only a small portion of the eastern slope of Mound 7 was spared total destruction, undoubtedly because of the house that was constructed on it (see Fig. 3.18).

Additional effects on the remains of Las Colinas have almost certainly resulted from the continuing processes accompanying the urbanization of the area: the excavation of foundations for houses and other structures, the digging of sewer trenches and holes for septic tanks, and the placement of underground cables and pipes of various sorts are all frequently occurring and are always destructive activities as far as subsurface archaeological materials are concerned. As always, the effects of pot hunting and outright vandalism cannot be overlooked. It is likely that digging in the ruins was and continues to be a recreational activity for some citizens. The photograph in Figure 3.32 shows a group of school children on a visit to Mound 3 sometime before 1930. Note that several of the children are carrying shovels.

*Figure 3.32.* Photograph of school children within the partially destroyed Mound 3, taken sometime around 1930.

In sum, the earliest effects on the remains of Las Colinas resulted from the cultivation of land and the construction of roads and houses. As a result of these processes, the destruction of the major mounds at the site and an unknown number of other features had begun by the 1880s, and in the case of the numbered mounds, was largely complete by 1930. Portions of at least two mounds have been preserved to the present, probably because residences were situated on them. As we shall see, it is probable that the overall effects of cultivation have been variable, and that while some features have been disturbed or destroyed, many others remain buried and intact below the plow zone. The continuing processes associated with urbanization have undoubtedly disturbed or destroyed many features.

## Postoccupational Processes Within the Corridor

The postoccupational processes that have operated specifically within the I-10 corridor are logically a microcosm of those described above for the general site area. Each sub-area, however, has experienced slightly different combinations of these processes and their effects, and since this information is relevant to the design of the testing program, it is useful to review each area separately. Table 3.3 summarizes the postoccupational processes that have occurred in each corridor sub-area, and lists the effects on archaeological materials where they are known or may be confidently speculated about.

*Area 1*

The principal processes affecting Area 1 have been long-term cultivation, the construction of historic canal segments and surface structures, and the excavation of holes for the installation of subsurface gasoline storage tanks.

This area was brought under cultivation by 1879, and in those areas that remained in use as fields, cultivation continued until at least 1940 (see Fig. 3.28 and Tables 3.2 and 3.3). The 1903 Reclamation Service map shows several small canal segments associated with the fields in Area 1 (see Fig. 2.11). By 1963, the area was no longer cultivated, and numerous structures had been constructed in the northern part of the area; at present, that part of the area is still occupied by a gas station, a truck terminal, and several other structures relating to the light industry that occupies the area. The remainder of the area has never been occupied by structures of any sort, and has remained as open fields since cultivation was abandoned.

The few trenches excavated in this area in 1968 revealed that there is a plow zone of approximately 30 cm to 40 cm,

TABLE 3.3

**Postoccupational Processes within the I-10 Corridor
and their Known Effects on Archaeological Materials**

| Sub-area | Postoccupational Processes | Known Effects on Archaeological Materials |
|---|---|---|
| 1 | Plowing and leveling for cultivation (from 1879)<br>Historic canal construction<br>Road and street construction<br>Construction of dwellings and other structures<br>Excavation of holes for gasoline storage tanks | Unknown; it may be logically assumed that such massive disturbance as that required for the installation of gasoline storage tanks would have destroyed any subsurface remains that may have existed in the affected area; plow zone of 30 cm to 40 cm is known to exist |
| 2 | Plowing and leveling for cultivation (from 1879)<br>Historic canal construction | Destruction of walls and floor of adobe-walled structure near Mound 8 (Feature 119; see Fig. 3.21); disturbance but not total destruction of cremations; disturbance but not total destruction of trash pit; possible total destruction of ballcourt; plow zone of 30 cm to 40 cm is known to exist |
| 3 | Construction of residence and associated structures<br>   excavation of basement of dwelling<br>Planting nonnative trees<br>Digging postholes for fenceposts | Destruction of major portions of the interior of Mound 8; destruction of surface features on Mound 8; root disturbance; indirectly the preservation of the bulk of Mound 8 |
| 4 | Plowing and leveling for cultivation (from 1879)<br>Construction of dwelling and other structures<br>Construction of concrete pads for trailers<br>Use of area for driveways and parking<br>Planting nonnative trees | Unknown; it may be expected that compaction would have occurred in those areas used consistently for driveways; excavation of sewer line and water line trenches would have produced subsurface disturbance |
| 5 | Plowing and leveling for cultivation (from 1877)<br>Road and street construction<br>House construction<br>Removal of houses and excavation of trenches to<br>   prevent vehicular access to area<br>Planting nonnative trees<br>Historic canal construction (Lateral 14)<br>Sewer line construction | Unknown; the excavation of trenches along the streets within the area may have disturbed subsurface features depending upon their depth; excavation of historic canal and sewer line trenches would have disturbed any remains in the areas affected |
| 6 | Plowing and leveling for cultivation (from 1877)<br>House construction (in extreme western end) | Unknown |

and we may expect that any surface remains that existed when plowing was begun would have long since been severely disturbed or completely destroyed.

*Area 2*

Like Area 1, Area 2 was brought under cultivation by 1879 and remained in use as agricultural land until at least the late 1950s (see Figs. 3.30 and 3.31). A historic canal was constructed in the area sometime before 1913, and a segment of this canal remains, forming the eastern boundary of the area. There is no evidence that any structures have ever been built in the area.

The extensive trenching of Area 2 in 1968 revealed that a 30 cm to 40 cm plow zone is present, and that plowing has disturbed some features and destroyed part of another. Of the six cremations recovered from this area in 1968, five had been disturbed and scattered somewhat by the plow. The sixth cremation was in place and intact, except that the bottom of the inverted bowl covering the vessel containing the cremation had been clipped off by the plow. Likewise, a small trash pit had been disturbed but not completely destroyed. The eastern end of Feature 119, an adobe-walled structure lying immediately east of Mound 8, had been completely destroyed, as neither the floor nor the walls of this structure could be traced beyond the point where the plowing had reached (see Figs. 3.21 and 3.30).

The edge of the unplowed area represents the former extent of the yard that surrounded the house built upon the mound.

If the ballcourt discussed above did ever exist in Area 2, it would appear on the basis of existing evidence that it has been completely destroyed by plowing.

## Area 3

As noted above, Area 3 subsumes Mound 8 and will not be dealt with during the testing. However, several important bits of information regarding the effects of postoccupational processes on remains in the immediate area may be discussed.

The house and associated structures that were built on the mound were surrounded by a yard, lined with nonnative trees including palms, tamarisk, and Texas umbrella or chinaberry. At least some of these trees appear to have been planted soon after the house was built in the 1880s, and the progress of their growth may be observed in the sequential photos of the house shown in Figures 3.23, 3.24, and 3.30. It is also clear that there was a fence around this yard during most of the occupation of the house. A driveway to 27th Avenue passed through this fence via a gate on the east side (Fig. 3.23).

The house on Mound 8 was unusual in that it had a basement, and this feature disturbed a large portion of the surface and interior of the mound. Disturbance was also caused by the construction of the privy, barn, and other outbuildings associated with the house. As has already been pointed out, however, it is likely that the lengthy occupation of the residence on Mound 8 to some degree insured the preservation of most of the mound. The significance of the presence of the house for present purposes is that the unplowed area which once constituted the yard around the house extends to the west into Area 4, and this portion of that area was spared the effects of the plow for this reason. So far as may be determined from the existing data, this is the only area of the corridor that was not plowed for long periods of time.

Also of interest is the fact that at least one of the trees shown in the early photos of Mound 8 is still standing (the palm immediately south of the former gate), and thus the probable location of postholes associated with the historic fence may be derived.

## Area 4

The postoccupational processes that have operated in Area 4 are fairly complex with respect to their possible effects on subsurface archaeological materials. The only area within the corridor which may be confidently shown not to have been plowed occupies the extreme eastern end of Area 4. In addition, the driveway leading up to the house was unplowed from at least 1936 on, and probably before that. It is possible that the area of the driveway was never plowed, as this would have prevented access to the house, which was there by the 1880s. It may also be that the entire area was not plowed as long as some of the other areas within the corridor. In Figures 3.23 and 3.24 the area immediately west of the house and outside the fenced yard does not appear to be under cultivation; it may be, of course, that the edge of the plowed area is outside the area covered by the photograph. The area does not appear to be under cultivation in either the 1936 or the 1940 aerial photographs, but remnants of plow furrows may be seen and the fields may have simply been lying fallow at the time of the photographs. We have no data regarding the depth of the plow zone in Area 4.

One house, another large structure, and concrete pads for trailers have all been constructed within Area 4. Any existing remains in the area of these features may be expected to have been disturbed by any subsurface excavation accomplished in the course of their construction. In addition, sewer lines laid along 27th Avenue in the extreme western portion of Area 4 are reported to have encountered buried remains. While the nature and depth of these remains is unknown, it may be assumed that the trenches required for these sewer lines would have done substantial damage to any subsurface materials that did exist.

## Area 5

Area 5, which lies at the eastern edge of Section 2, T1N R2E, was initially brought under cultivation in 1877 and was cultivated through at least the 1940s (see Fig. 3.28). Associated with the cultivation of the area was the Lateral 14 canal, which paralleled the present course of 27th Avenue on its western side and which therefore cut north and south through the extreme edge of Area 4. A housing development was built on the area during the 1950s with several short street segments associated with these houses.

The houses were removed during the late 1970s, and shallow trenches were excavated around the former house lots to prevent vehicular access to the area. As has already been noted, these trenches brought up abundant cultural material, and probably disturbed any shallow features that may have been present. Since we do not know the nature of the features that may exist or the strata in which they originate, the exact nature and degree of the disturbance is unknown.

## Area 6

Area 6 is also within the portion of Section 2 brought under cultivation by 1877, and the bulk of the area was cultivated through the 1960s (see Fig. 3.29). A small historic canal segment shown on the 1903 Reclamation Service map may fall within the western end of Area 6. There is no evidence to suggest that any structures were ever erected in Area 6, with the exception of a small area in the extreme western end, just east of 30th Drive. These houses were constructed at approximately the same time as those in Area 5. We have no evidence that demonstrates the former existence of archaeological features and materials in Area 6, so the effects of cultivation and the construction of houses on any existing remains is unknown.

## Postoccupational Processes at Other Sites: Cultivation

While it is clear that the postoccupational processes that have operated in the corridor are quite varied, it is also obvious that cultivation is the activity that has occurred most consistently across the corridor sub-areas of concern. With the exception of the area around Mound 8, it appears that the entire corridor was under cultivation at one time or another. The other activities that have had, or may be expected to have had, effects on subsurface remains may be isolated in at least their spatial dimension. We know where houses have been, where canals were dug, where sewers were laid, and so forth, and thus may have quite specific expectations as to *where* subsurface disturbance resulting from these activities has occurred.

The overall effects of cultivation, however, are less well understood. Some information is available from Area 2, and it has been shown that a substantial plow zone exists in Area 1, but the data from the site with respect to the expected effects of long-term cultivation are limited. It is useful, therefore, to consult data from other sites in the area in an effort to establish some more specific idea of the effects of cultivation on subsurface archaeological remains. Some data are also available on the efficacy of various methods used to locate buried features in plowed areas.

Recent excavations directed by Dr. David R. Wilcox of Arizona State University at the site of Los Hornos provide a variety of information concerning the effects of cultivation. The area of the site that was tested included some 60 acres around the former location of a platform mound, which was completely graded down sometime during the 1950s (Nelson 1981). The area of concern had been cultivated for approximately the same length of time as the areas at Las Colinas within the I-10 corridor. A wheel-trencher was used to excavate trenches in order to locate and record subsurface materials.

More than eight hundred features were discovered either wholly or partially undisturbed below the plow zone, including pit houses, coursed caliche structures, a ballcourt, hornos or ovens, trash pits of varying sizes, cremation, and inhumations. The plow zone was consistently 30 cm to 40 cm deep. For the most part, the features were initially encountered either at or just below the interface between the plow zone and deeper undisturbed deposits. The ballcourt discovered had been partially destroyed, with the top of the banks forming the sides of the court and the end courts removed by plowing. The central part of the court and its truncated sides remained. Excellent data regarding the nature and distribution of features at the site was obtained from Los Hornos, primarily through the profiling of the excavated trenches.

At AZ U:9:46 (ASM), a dual component site consisting of pit houses, associated nonarchitectural features, and canal segments, a 50-cm plow zone was present in an area that had been plowed for some 70 years (Herskovitz 1974). Again, the features were discovered at the bottom of or slightly below the plow zone, and some were disturbed while others were intact. Six houses, five canal segments, and 16 nonarchitectural features were recorded. Two of the six houses had been intruded by plowing, and the banks of the canal segments discovered had been leveled and removed. These features were discovered using a backhoe, and it is of some interest that the density of surface materials was not in this case a good indicator of subsurface features. Only a minimal sherd and lithic scatter was present on the surface, and the initial trenching was undertaken to locate canals visible on aerial photographs. Four canal segments seen on aerial photographs were thus documented, but all of the houses and other features as well as an additional canal segment were encountered by backhoe trenches.

At the site of Pueblo del Monte (U:9:39, ASU), a ballcourt which was observed on the surface in 1929 was not observable in 1970 and had apparently been completely obliterated at least in part by plowing (Weaver 1977). The area where the court was once recorded was not excavated, and whether portions of it remained intact under the surface is therefore unknown. Several other features observed in 1929 could not be seen in 1970, and their destruction may be attributed in part to cultivation. At least a portion of a large trash mound did survive (Weaver 1977).

The data summarized above are by no means the only information available, and this brief and selective review is not intended to be exhaustive. It is sufficient, however, to support several general conclusions regarding the effects of long-term cultivation on archaeological materials within the area, and these, in turn, bear on the formulation of the testing program outlined below:

1. Some features survive the plow and some do not; as noted, the survival of buried features depends upon a variety of factors. There is abundant evidence, however, that archaeological features and materials have survived decades of plowing, and may remain either wholly or partially intact below the plow zone.

2. Most subsurface archaeological features discovered in areas that have been plowed occur at or just below the interface of the plow zone with undisturbed deposits.

3. The plow zone in the Phoenix area appears to range between 30 cm and 50 cm, with an average depth of 40 cm; this depth is well within the range of the plow zone documented in Areas 1 and 2 at Las Colinas.

4. The use of backhoe and a wheel-trencher have both been successful discovery techniques in formerly cultivated areas.

5. Features that were on or near the surface of the ground when plowing was initiated are likely to have been substantially disturbed if not completely destroyed.

6. The absence of surface features and materials is not an absolute indicator of the absence of buried features, and such features *may* occur in areas where the surface density of materials is low.

With respect to the corridor area of concern, it may be suggested that if unknown subsurface features and deposits exist, and if they have not been disturbed or destroyed by activities other than cultivation, it is likely that they remain wholly or partially intact beneath the plow zone; further, it may be expected that these features will be initially encountered at or just below the interface of the plow zone with the deeper, undisturbed deposits, or in the case of Areas 1 and 2, at approximately 30 cm to 40 cm below the present ground surface.

## Summary

The available data on the site of Las Colinas have been reviewed and summarized in terms of the preliminary research questions outlined above. The former nature and extent of the site have been discussed, and the relationship of the site to the I-10 corridor established both in general terms and with respect to those materials that have been documented within the corridor segment of concern. A summary of postoccupational processes operating in the area of the site and specifically within the corridor has been presented, and the various effects of those processes discussed. It is appropriate to conclude this section dealing with the preliminary research with several observations regarding the overall character of Las Colinas and its relationship to other sites in the area.

The existing data suggest that Las Colinas was a large Classic period site having at least four platform mounds. Three of these mounds were surrounded by compound walls, two of them by a single wall that is one of, if not the, largest such feature recorded. Mound 8 appears to have been the smallest of the four features that may be confidently called platform mounds, being perhaps a quarter of the size of Mound 7. Mound 8 may or may not have had a compound wall around it. The nature of the other eight mounds numbered by Turney (1929) is less well known, but it may be stated with some confidence that in addition to the platform mounds, the ruins of roomblocks, trash mounds, pit houses, borrow pits, cremations, and inhumations were also present at the site. A ballcourt is reported as having been located to the east of Mound 8, but the evidence for its actual existence is equivocal. Little is known of the overall distribution of features other than the mounds. There is some evidence of a Preclassic occupation in the area of Las Colinas, specifically around Mound 8.

By virtue of the individual features known to have existed at the site, Las Colinas is not terribly different from any one of several other large Classic period sites in the Salt River Valley. Several characteristics of the site, however, argue for its special nature.

It is clear that Las Colinas was one of the larger Classic period sites in the area. If the distribution of features shown on the early maps of the area may be taken as any indicator of relative site size, only Los Muertos, Mesa Grande, Pueblo Grande, and La Ciudad were roughly equal in extent. While we may question the specific accuracy of these maps, the identity of Las Colinas as a major site seems indubitable.

This conclusion is also supported by what may be the most striking feature of the site, and the characteristic that gave it its name: the unusual number of large mounds. None of the other sites shown on the early maps of the area even approach having the total of 10 shown for Las Colinas. In fact, most have only 1 (Turney 1929). This fact is even more significant when we consider that at least 4 of those mounds, and possibly more, were platform mounds. The closest contender here for a similar number of such features is Casa Grande which, if we stretch the definition and include the basal floor of the Great House and assume that Compound B had 2, would have a total of 3. Unless we count the feature contained in Group 1, Los Muertos does not appear to have had a platform mound at all.

Much of this data, of course, is speculation based on maps that may in many ways be considered suspect in terms of their accuracy and completeness. Nonetheless, the apparent variability in the kinds and quantities of specialized features recorded at Classic period sites would seem a fruitful topic for investigation in the interest of gaining a further understanding of the nature and structure of Classic period Hohokam society. There is little doubt that Las Colinas occupied a special place in that society, and as this general conclusion anticipates the problem framework to be employed in the proposed testing, we may logically move to that section of this document.

# Proposed Testing

Having reviewed the available data on Las Colinas, we may now present the questions to be addressed during the testing program and discuss the methods to be used in collecting the data relevant to those questions. The discussion that follows establishes the general framework in which the research problems may be best understood, delineates the specific questions to be addressed during the testing, and documents the general and specific methodology to be employed.

## Research Questions

At the most general level, the questions to be addressed during the proposed testing at Las Colinas may be seen as relating to a single, broad topic: the morphology of Classic period Hohokam sites. Morphology is used here to refer to the kinds, quantities, distributions, and arrangements of features and materials within sites, or put more succinctly, the internal structure of sites (Struever 1968). Normally included under the even broader rubric of settlement pattern studies, the individual and comparative study of the morphological characteristics of sites has been used widely in the investigation of various aspects of prehistoric social and political organization as well as other topics (Adams and Nissen 1972; Bluhm 1960; Chang 1962; Hammond 1975; Meggers 1955; Parsons 1972; Plog 1974; Struever 1968; Trigger 1968; Willey 1953, 1955).

Given what is already known of Las Colinas, this is hardly the only topic that might be addressed. The primary advantages gained through the use of the concept of site morphology are twofold. First, the general concerns and classes of data referred to by the concept mesh nicely with the managerial problems to be dealt with in the testing. Second, the use of the concept allows the quite specific and basic questions to be addressed during the testing to be integrated with several current themes in the study of Hohokam prehistory. Thus, in the process of providing the necessary managerial information, small trenches may be seen in the light of larger issues, and the broader scientific relevance of the data obtained from the testing program may be established and fully exploited.

One recent emphasis in Hohokam studies has been on a set of interrelated concerns dealing with the nature and development of Hohokam social and political organization, frequently viewed from a regional perspective (Doyel 1976, 1978; Gumerman and Spoerl 1978; Plog 1978; Teague 1981; Wilcox 1979, 1980; Wilcox and Shenk 1977). An important piece in the mosaic of problems that may be logically generated from these general concerns is the question of the social and political organization that functioned within individual communities or groupings of communities

(Doyel 1974, 1976; Wilcox 1979, 1980; Wilcox and Shenk 1977).

The information derived from the preliminary research documented above should be sufficient to demonstrate the importance and appropriateness of the site of Las Colinas as a locus in which to pursue the further study and understanding of the site-specific aspects of Hohokam social and political organization. Mound 8 represents one of the few examples of a well-documented, well-dated platform mound and immediate surrounding areas. Because of the developmental sequence of construction contained in Mound 8 and its associated features, there is an excellent opportunity to study the changes in character and use of space that occurred there, and thus to derive inferences about the organizational aspects of the prehistoric groups that wrought those changes. Consequently, the value of the data that may be obtained from the proposed testing is greatly enhanced by virtue of the simple physical proximity of the corridor areas to Mound 8. The information gained from the testing may be related to the touchstone of Mound 8, thence to the larger questions of Hohokam social and political organization. The notion of site morphology provides the conceptual bridge between these larger issues and the rather limited testing proposed at this time.

This does not mean that the problems of Classic period socio-political organization will be solved, or even studied directly, for the study of site morphology is *not* the same thing as the study of prehistoric organizational forms. It is *through* the examination and analytic manipulation of the morphological characteristics of sites—guided by particular questions and within particular theoretical frameworks—that inferences regarding the organizational aspects of past societies may be successfullly derived. Further, it should be noted that the proposed testing will not establish a complete picture of the morphology of the unknown areas around Mound 8, even within the corridor. To accomplish this would require a full-scale data recovery program involving broad horizontal exposure of large areas, a strategy clearly inappropriate at this time. What the testing may be legitimately expected to provide is some limited but nonetheless important data regarding the relative distribution of features and materials within the corridor and thus in the vicinity of Mound 8. Viewed in this way, the data obtained from the proposed testing will provide a firmer foundation for the continuing investigation of Hohokam social and political organization as it is revealed in the morphological characteristics of the Mound 8 area, and therefore of Las Colinas and Classic period sites in general.

Specifically, very little is known of the internal structure of large Classic period sites. With the exceptions of Los Muertos and Casa Grande, few major sites have been mapped in a manner that would allow the comparative study of their internal structure. How are lesser features distributed around platform mounds? Is the distribution of features within large sites more or less continuous, or are there large areas of "empty" space? What features occur in close proximity to platform mounds, and what do these features tell us about the way in which the space was used? What changes in these distributions occur during the Classic period? All these questions are important to understanding the internal structure of the study of organizational features. And, all of these questions are at least touched upon by the proposed testing of the I-10 corridor. With this general perspective in mind, the following research questions may be posed and briefly discussed:

1.  *What is the nature and distribution of subsurface materials within the corridor as revealed by the proposed testing?*

This is the most general and basic question to be addressed, bearing on both the managerial purposes and scientific goals of the testing. All the data collected will relate in one way or another to this question. We may expect that two specific forms of this question might be answered during the testing:

1a.  *Was there a compound wall around Mound 8?*

1b.  *Are there additional cremations in the area southeast of Mound 8?*

2.  *What is the temporal distribution of cultural features and materials encountered in the corridor sub-areas?*

The dating of any materials encountered during the testing has obvious significance, bearing on the question of the distribution of any Preclassic occupation in the Mound 8 area as well as on the distribution of any Classic period materials that are, therefore, comparable to those from the Mound 8 area. Relevant data for answering this question will include ceramic materials, stratigraphic relationships, and possibly materials suitable for absolute dating. Because of the self-imposed restrictions on the horizontal exposure of subsurface materials, the opportunity to obtain ceramic materials and materials suitable for chronometric dating will be limited.

3.  *How does the vertical distribution of cultural features and materials, and noncultural deposits, relate to the basal level of Mound 8?*

This question relates to a variety of issues, including the degree to which the area away from Mound 8 has been leveled by plowing, and the former location of the aboriginal surface as represented by the basal level of Mound 8. This, in turn, is related to the question of whether or not surface features once existed and have now been destroyed by cultivation. The data necessary to answer this question are easily obtainable, since a permanent datum set at the elevation of the basal level of the mound was placed during the 1968 excavations.

4.  *What may be said about the prehistoric use of those areas where no cultural features or materials are encountered?*

In light of the general problem orientation outlined above, it is clear that the failure to encounter cultural features and materials during the testing will be as significant as their discovery, for even sterile trenches will inform on the distribution of features. In addition, some data may be collected that have the potential to reveal the former nature of such areas beyond their identity as empty space. Pollen and soil analysis will be the means for attempting to study this question.

5.  *What evidence exists that surface features were once present and have been wholly or partially destroyed by cultivation?*

Related in part to question 3, this question may be answered by determining the strata in which cultural materials are observed, and by documenting the relationships between culture-bearing and sterile strata. These relationships may be established by careful profiling of trenches.

6.  *What may be inferred from the characteristics and distributions of the cultural and non-culture bearing deposits and features recorded about the ways in which the space around Mound 8 was used?*

This final question is broadly synthetic and looks forward to the analysis and interpretation of the data to be collected during the testing. It also relates the entire testing program to the general problem framework outlined above.

### Classes of Data to be Collected

The data necessary to answer these questions fall into two major categories: (1) relational data and (2) artifacts and samples of noncultural materials.

Relational data refer to the information contained in profiles, maps, drawings and the like, and will be the most important for the testing program. The emphasis on relational data is determined by the research questions and by the goal of keeping the disturbance to subsurface remains to a minimum. Less important will be artifactual data, since only a limited number of artifacts may be expected to result from the methods to be employed in the testing (see below). Nonartifactual samples will be collected and will be important in the interpretation of areas lacking cultural materials.

If the appropriate situations present themselves, soil samples will be taken for pollen extraction and soil analysis.

The ability to successfully interpret the results of palynological analysis depends in large part upon the ability to interpret the stratigraphy from which the samples are taken. Thus, the number of samples to be taken for analysis will depend on the nature of the stratigraphy encountered in the various test trenches. Determination of samples to be taken will be made in the field in consultation with a trained palynologist. The consultant will also be responsible for the analysis and interpretation of any samples taken.

## Methodology

The principal field methods to be employed during the testing will include remote sensing (Subsurface Interface Radar), backhoe trenching, and some hand excavation. These general methods will be deployed individually and in combination in the five corridor sub-areas in order to provide the data required by the research questions. The discussion below details: (1) the general guidelines to be followed in the use of each of the general methods to be applied, and (2) the specific combination of methodologies to be employed in each of the corridor sub-areas.

### Subsurface Interface Radar

In keeping with the overall goal of providing the required information concerning the distribution of subsurface features and materials within the corridor, with minimum disturbance to those resources, several methods of nondestructive testing were considered. Subsurface Interface Radar has been selected for use.

This type of remote sensing works by directing high frequency impulses of energy into the ground and receiving the reflection of those impulses from interface zones within the ground (such as between soil types, soil and rock, and soil and clay). The readings produced are recorded on tapes and may be played back at a slower speed than that at which they were moved over the ground, thus providing for the necessarily detailed analysis of the results. The method has not been substantially tested in the arid Southwest, but has achieved good results in locating and even identifying subsurface features in the eastern United States (Roberts, in press).

This method is particularly appropriate for use at Las Colinas for several reasons. First, the basic stratigraphy of the corridor area is well known, as is the nature and location of former subsurface disturbances. The locations of former houses are known and are represented on scale maps (see below), and the areas of plowing have been documented. Thus the interpretation of the results of radar survey will be easier than in areas where these variables are unknown. Second, the location of at least one buried fea-

ture is known (Feature 39, east of Mound 8), and half of the feature has been excavated, so that a baseline for the interpretation of results may be established with respect to a specifically known feature. Third, the method is relatively quick, so the results may be used in structuring the use of other testing methods. Fourth, the necessary equipment is relatively portable and is well suited for use in open, flat areas such as those represented by the corridor sub-areas. Finally, the use of radar will be a potential source of additional control over the backhoe trenching to be accomplished.

The method does require personnel trained in the use of the equipment and in the interpretation of the results, so a consultant qualified in the use of the equipment will be hired for the testing program. The appropriate spacing of the radar transects and all other aspects of the radar survey will be determined by the consultant, in accordance with the goals of the testing as defined by the research questions.

The specific use of radar survey in each corridor sub-area is discussed below.

### Backhoe Trenching

The use of a backhoe to locate subsurface features and materials has been a common and effective practice in the excavation of Hohokam archaeological sites. Especially in areas where no indications of subsurface remains may be found, and where confirmation or denial of the apparent lack of materials is desired, the backhoe is one of the more useful tools available to the archaeologist.

The principal difficulties in the use of the backhoe are: (1) the fact that it is subject to only limited control, which varies considerably with the individual operator and which will result in some damage to features and materials encountered, and (2) the fact that the machine produces trenches with rough sides that must be faced up before the profile may be successfully inspected for stratigraphy and features. Nonetheless, these shortcomings will be overcome with proper attention, including the use of the radar survey discussed above and adherence to the explicit guidelines for backhoe trenching already outlined.

Most of the trenches to be excavated during the proposed testing will employ a backhoe. The specific number and placement of trenches for each corridor sub-area is discussed below. The following guidelines will be observed for *all* backhoe trenches to be excavated:

1. Before starting any trenching, the appropriate utility companies will be contacted to insure that buried cables, pipes, and the like are not present.
2. A 24-inch bucket will be used on the backhoe to allow sufficient room in the trenches for facing up and profiling.
3. At least a three-person crew will be used in conjunction with the backhoe: one examining the trench

and backdirt for cultural materials, the other two facing up each trench as it is completed.

4. In those areas where systematic backhoe trenches are to be placed, off-set parallel lines of north-south trenches 30 m in length will be excavated, with the trenches in a single line separated by a distance of 45 m. The north-south lines of trenches will be separated by a distance of 15 m. This pattern will be followed in all areas where the backhoe is to be used, except in Sub-area 6, where several additional trenches will be excavated (see discussion below).

5. Any trench encountering cultural features or artifactual materials will be discontinued. Then the appropriate section of the trench will be faced and profiled, with the stratigraphic relationships of the features, or materials, or both recorded. If examination of the profile reveals that the artifactual materials are located *only* in the plow zone, then the trench will be continued; if examination of the profile reveals in situ deposits extending below the plow zone, the trench will be discontinued and the next trench begun. The single exception to this rule will be canal segments. It is unlikely that a canal profile would be seen in the trench wall before the trench was faced up, and the overall integrity of a canal segment would not be compromised by having a trench cut across it. If either prehistoric or historic canals are intersected, they will be profiled in detail.

6. It follows logically from the previous point that the depth of trenches will vary according to whether cultural features and materials are encountered and according to the strata in which those features or materials occur. In those trenches where no cultural materials or features are encountered, or where the materials are restricted to the plow zone, the trenches will be excavated to a depth of 3 m or to the caliche substrate where it is present. The excavation of all trenches through caliche to an arbitrary depth would be time-consuming and unnecessary for the purposes of the proposed testing. However, portions of selected trenches will be excavated to a depth of 3 m. The number and selection of the trenches to be excavated to this depth is discussed for each corridor sub-area.

7. Any cultural feature or artifactual materials encountered will be left in place to the degree practicable; in cases where the absolute or stratigraphic integrity of a feature is severely threatened (for example, in the rare case of a cremation falling out of a trench wall), it will be removed and its context fully recorded; in any case where a question arises concerning proper procedure, the State Historic Preservation Officer will be consulted before proceeding.

8. Backdirt from the backhoe trenches wll be continually examined for artifactual materials; if such material is observed, the appropriate section of the backdirt will be screened and the materials collected. To the degree possible, the materials' association with features and deposits will be recorded. In addition, portions of each trench will be systematically screened in the following manner: approximately 1.5 cu m of dirt from each trench will be screened, divided equally among three places in the trench (approximately 0.5 cu m from the first few bucketfuls excavated, 0.5 cu m from the middle of the trench, and 0.5 cu m from the end of the trench). To the degree possible, the backdirt from the plow zone will be screened separately from deeper deposits, so that approximately 0.75 cu m of dirt will be screened from each of these two basic units in each trench.

9. In the absence of cultural materials and variations in the natural stratigraphy, a 2-m segment of each trench will be profiled. In those trenches lacking cultural materials but exhibiting significant variability in natural stratigraphy, an appropriate number of additional profiles will be drawn to adequately record the variability. Each trench will also be photographed.

10. The bottoms of trenches will be marked with sheets of plastic, and the trenches will be backfilled at the end of each day's work.

11. The locations of the trenches excavated, the profiles drawn, and any samples taken will be plotted on maps of an appropriate scale, so that the locations of any relationships between all trenches will be recorded. All vertical measurements will be tied into the permanent datum placed to the west of Mound 8 during the 1968 excavations (this elevation is equal to the basal levels of Mound 8).

## Hand Excavation

In Sub-area 5, the use of hand-excavated trenches is called for. Those trenches to be excavated by hand will be treated in the following manner:

1. The trenches will be excavated in levels of natural stratigraphy if present, and in arbitrary 10-cm levels if not.

2. All material from the hand-excavated trenches will be screened through ¼-inch mesh.

3. The same guidelines for profiling and mapping backhoe trenches will be followed for hand-excavated trenches.

4. Since one of the important questions to be answered in Sub-area 5 is whether the cultural materials observed there are present only in the plow zone, or are coming from deeper, undisturbed deposits, it will be necessary to excavate these trenches below the plow zone. The absolute depth of each trench may be expected to vary, depending upon the nature of the stratigraphy and materials encountered.

## Methods to be Employed Because of Requests of the Advisory Council

Requests have been made by the Federal Highway Administration regarding two specific techniques to be employed in the excavation of backhoe trenches during the testing. These requests have been made in response to criticism of our proposal and other Papago Freeway-related work by the Advisory Council on Historic Preservation, the Interagency Archaeological Services, and other interested parties. These two requests are:

1. That a consistent portion of the dirt removed from *every* backhoe trench be screened even if there is no evidence for the presence of cultural materials;

2. That some unspecified number of backhoe trenches be excavated to an arbitrary depth of 3 m, again regardless of whether there is any evidence for the presence of cultural materials.

These are neither prudent nor logical archaeological procedures, are not likely to produce any relevant information, are time-consuming and inefficient, and were *not* included as an integral part of the research design presented here. In the first case, the materials that may result from such screening may only be understood and interpreted in the context of the strata from which they originate, and provisions for the observation and recording of such relationships have been included in the guidelines for the proposed trenching. Further, it is unlikely that substantial amounts of material coming out of backhoe trenches would escape the notice of the individuals assigned specifically to look for

such materials. In the second case, given what is already known of the basic stratigraphy within the corridor and of the vertical distribution of cultural features and materials, the 2-m depth provided for in the guidelines is quite appropriate. Cultural deposits of 3 m or found *at* a depth of 3 m are rare, and the conditions documented above for the corridor make it unlikely that such deposits will be encountered. We do not wish to excavate such useless trenches or screen obviously sterile backdirt, but have included provisions for doing so at the request of the Federal Highway Administration.

With the exception of these two items, we consider all of the proposed testing to be well considered, appropriate, and likely to produce the information relevant to managerial needs and to the research questions.

## Corridor Sub-Areas

The following section details the specific set of techniques to be employed in each corridor sub-area. The locations of each area may be seen in Figure 3.33, and the discussion of each of the areas is accompanied by one or more maps showing the proposed trenches and other relevant features of the areas. In every case, the trenches shown on these maps are *the maximum number that will be excavated, providing no cultural materials or features are encountered in any trench.* The quantitative data relating to each area are given following the discussion of the proposed methodology.

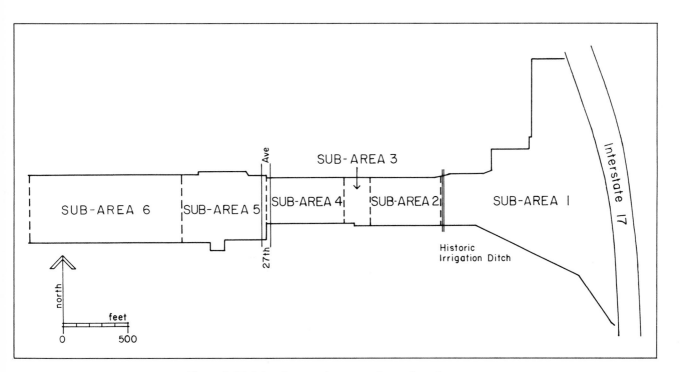

*Figure 3.33.* Map showing location of corridor sub-areas.

*Sub-area 1*

From the preliminary research documented above, it would appear that the principal postoccupational factor affecting most of Sub-area 1 has been long-term plowing. The exception to this is the presence of several buildings located in the northern part of the area. Some of the area is, therefore, unavailable for testing at the present time (see Fig. 3.34a). The existing data give no indication of any cultural features or materials within the area, with the exceptions of the probable presence of one or more historic canal segments and the remote possibility of a prehistoric canal segment. The appropriate method for testing the area, then, is a systematic one, and will consist of the use of two of the general methods outlined above.

First, a radar survey of the area will be accomplished and the results analyzed. Those areas producing readings that suggest the presence of subsurface materials will be flagged. The pattern of backhoe trenching shown in Figures 3.34a and 3.34b will then be initiated, with particular care taken in those areas targeted by the radar survey.

If any substantial area of subsurface features is indicated by the radar survey, the edges of this area will be trenched first, so that the extent of the distribution may be established with minimum disturbance.

The number of trench segments represented on Figures 3.34a and 3.34b is the *maximum* number that will be excavated; should any cultural materials be encountered, the aggregate length of the trenches shown would be reduced, according to the general guidelines for backhoe trenching outlined above. Because of the presence of buildings and paved lots, the excavation of trenches in the northern part of Sub-area 1 may be eliminated from the testing. At least five trenches in Sub-area 1 will be partially excavated to a depth of 3 m. The selection of these trenches will be a field decision, based on the stratigraphy encountered.

The quantitative data for Sub-area 1 are based on the area that will be dealt with (the open fields), and all calculations have been made on the basis of this area. Those data are:

Area of Sub-area 1: 84,742 square meters (21 acres)
Area covered by 1968 trenches: Negligible
Area to be covered by testing if full pattern is accomplished: 797 square meters
Percentage of surface area covered: 0.94 percent

*Sub-area 2*

As noted, the trenching accomplished in Sub-area 2 in 1968 established the existence of subsurface features, and also indicated that the overall feature density as revealed by those trenches is low. In Sub-area 2, therefore, it is necessary to test only those portions of the area not covered by the earlier trenching.

The testing of Sub-area 2 will proceed in the manner outlined for Sub-area 1: a radar survey of the area will be accomplished, targeting possible areas of subsurface features. The same systematic pattern of trenches used for Sub-area 1 will be employed, with the placement of the trenches as seen in Figure 3.35.

In addition to the excavation of new trenches, several segments of the 1968 trenches will be reopened and profiled to provide comparative data relating to the research questions. Two trenches in Sub-area 2 will be excavated to a depth of 3 m. The selection of these trenches will be a field decision based on the stratigraphy encountered.

The number of trench segments represented on Figure 3.35 is the maximum number that will be excavated if *no* cultural materials are encountered in *any* trench; should any cultural materials be encountered, the aggregate length of the trenches will be reduced according to the general guidelines for the backhoe trenching outlined above.

The quantitative data for Sub-area 2 are:

Area of Sub-area 2: 16,813 square meters (4.2 acres)
Area covered by 1968 trenches: 390 square meters
Percentage of surface area covered by 1968 trenches: 2.32 percent
Area to be covered by testing if full pattern is accomplished: 66.4 square meters
Percentage of surface area to be covered by testing: 0.25 percent
Combined percentage of surface area covered: 2.57 percent

*Sub-area 3*

Sub-area 3 includes Mound 8 and the area covered in the 1968 excavations, and will not be included in the present testing. Sub-area 3 is pictured in Figure 3.36 so that some idea of the relationship of Mound 8 to the other areas may be gained, and so that the extent of the unplowed area around Mound 8 may be seen.

The quantitative data for Sub-area 3 are:

Area of Sub-area 3: 8303 square meters (2.05 acres)

*Sub-area 4*

Sub-area 4 is potentially the most sensitive with respect to the possible disturbance of subsurface materials and will be handled with appropriate care. This will be the last of the five sub-areas to be dealt with (see below), so that the information gained from the other areas may be used to assemble the most prudent testing plan possible for Sub-area 4.

We know that there is at least one feature in Sub-area 4, the unexcavated portion of Feature 39 (see Fig. 3.21). There is also a considerable rise in the eastern end of the area, and it is likely that this rise covers at least some subsurface features, possibly a compound wall associated with Mound 8. The rest of the area is an unknown quantity, but buried materials have been observed immediately to the west in Sub-area 5. Since the materials in Sub-area 5 have resulted from the excavation of trenches, it may be assumed that they represent buried materials. Thus, Sub-area 4 is surrounded on at least three sides by areas that are known, or likely to have, subsurface materials.

Radar survey of the area will be accomplished, and the possible areas of subsurface features flagged. Depending upon the results of this radar survey and the results of the testing in Sub-area 5, the necessity for and appropriate number of trenches in Sub-area 4 will be determined. If the testing in Sub-area 5 indicates that the cultural materials are generally restricted to the plow zone, and *if* the radar survey shows *no* conclusive indications of subsurface features in Sub-area 4, then some backhoe trenching may be necessary. If this proves to be the case, then the same systematic pattern of trenching used for other areas will be employed. This pattern is shown in Figure 3.37 and represents the maximum number of trenches to be placed in the area. It should be stressed that the trenches shown in Figure 3.37 are provisional, and their excavation will depend on the results of the radar survey and the results of testing in Sub-area 5. Depending upon the outcome of these activities, the need for, and number of, trenches in Sub-area 4 will be determined in consultation with the SHPO. The aggregate length of trenches shown in Figure 3.37 may thus be reduced, according to the results of the Sub-area 5 testing, the radar survey, and the general guidelines for backhoe trenching outlined above.

Quantitative data on Sub-area 4 are:
Area of Sub-area 4: 16,723 square meters (4.13 acres)
Area to be covered by testing: 228 square meters
Percentage of surface area potentially covered: 1.36 percent

*Sub-area 5*

In addition to having been plowed for a long period of time and having the Lateral 14 canal cut through its extreme eastern edge, Sub-area 5 was the locus of a compact housing development. The former locations of the houses may be seen on Figure 3.38. It is also known that abundant cultural material is present in and along a series of shallow trenches dug around most of the area encompassing the former house lots. Thus the probability that subsurface deposits exist in Sub-area 5 is high. Because the area has already been disturbed by the above-mentioned trenches, these disturbed areas will be used for the testing in order to keep further disturbance to a minimum.

Radar survey will again be used, but because of the probable former existence of water lines, gas lines, and the like beneath and between the former houses, and possibly other

kinds of disturbance, it may be expected that the results of the radar survey will be difficult to intepret. In addition, it is necessary to know what strata are producing the abundant materials. Are they coming from the plow zone *and* from undisturbed deposits beneath, or from completely undisturbed deposits that have only recently been intruded by the trenches? To answer these questions, the existing trenches will be divided into 10-m segments. The surface around each segment for a meter on either side will then be surface collected to provide some quantitative measure of the density of materials coming out of the trenches and to provide ceramic materials for purposes of dating. Then every third 10-m segment will be cleaned and faced by hand. Once these trenches have been cleaned and profiled, the need to excavate deeper will be determined. These trenches will be excavated at least to the bottom of the plow zone, so that the relationships described above may be observed.

The location of the trenches shown in Figure 3.39 is not precise, as they have not been placed on any available maps. Their location, however, and therefore the position of the proposed trenches, is a good approximation, and the maximum number of trenches in Sub-area 5 will not exceed that shown on this map.

The quantitative data on Sub-area 5 are:
Area of Sub-area 5: 25,084 square meters (6.2 acres)
Area to be covered by proposed trenches: 108.9 square meters
Percentage of surface area to be covered by testing: 0.43 percent

*Sub-area 6*

Only a small part of Sub-area 6 is available for testing at the present time, because most of the area has not been acquired. Thus the testing will be restricted to a small area at the western end of Area 6. This area was once occupied by a series of houses, the former locations of which may be seen in Figure 3.40. Until the 1950s when these dwellings were constructed, this area had been continuously plowed since 1877. There is no existing information to suggest the probability of subsurface features and materials in the area.

Given these circumstances, the same method of testing employed in Sub-area 1 will be used: an initial radar survey will be accomplished, and any areas of possible subsurface features flagged. However, because of the probable subsurface disturbance associated with these houses and the resulting difficulties in interpreting the results of the radar survey, backhoe trenching will also be employed. The overall pattern represented in Sub-area 1 will be duplicated and will be augmented by the addition of several east-west trench segments to increase the coverage in this area.

The pattern and number of trenches shown is the maximum that will be excavated, providing no subsurface features or materials are encountered. Portions of two of the

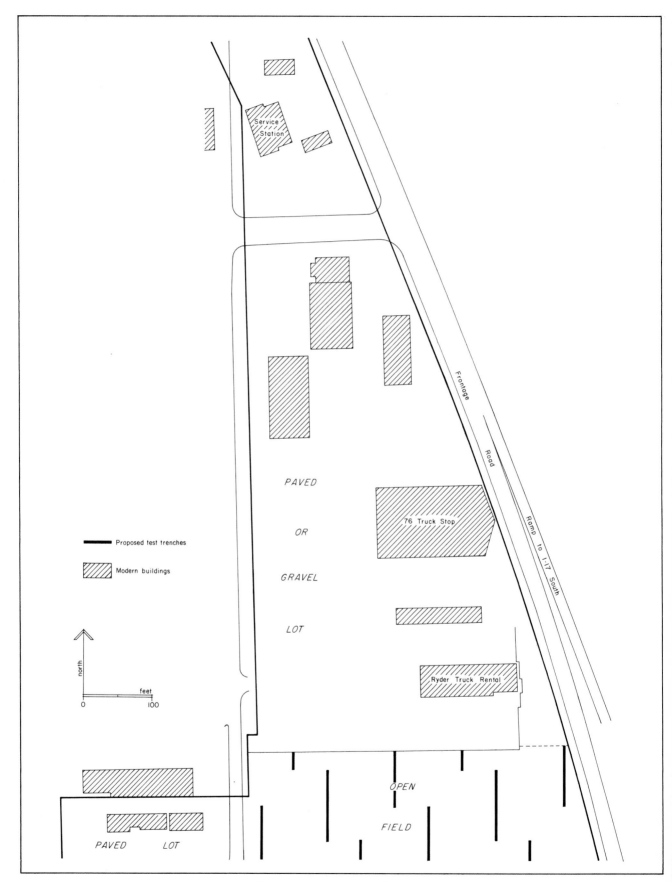

*Figure 3.34a.* Corridor Sub-area 1.

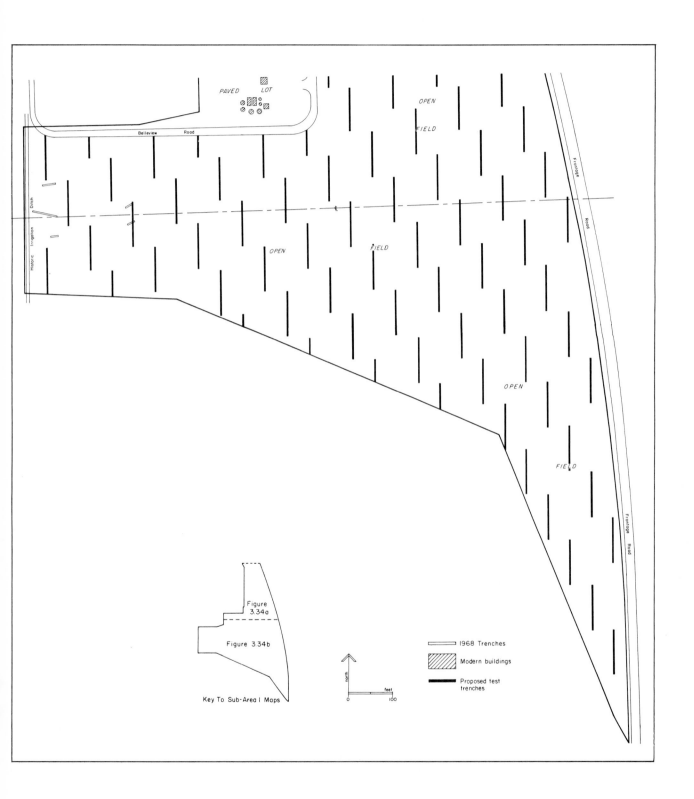

*Figure 3.34b.* Corridor Sub-area 1.

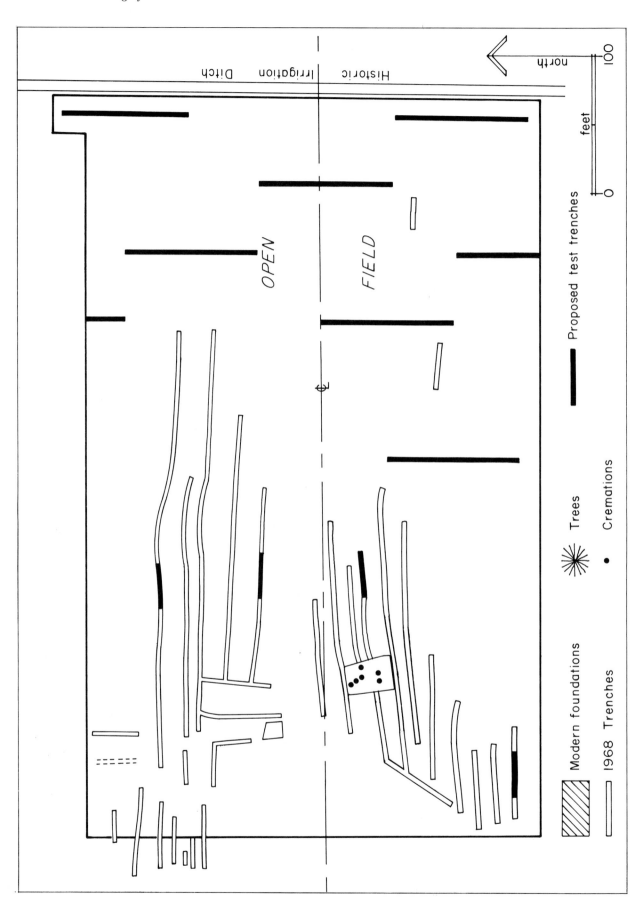

*Figure 3.35.* Corridor Sub-area 2.

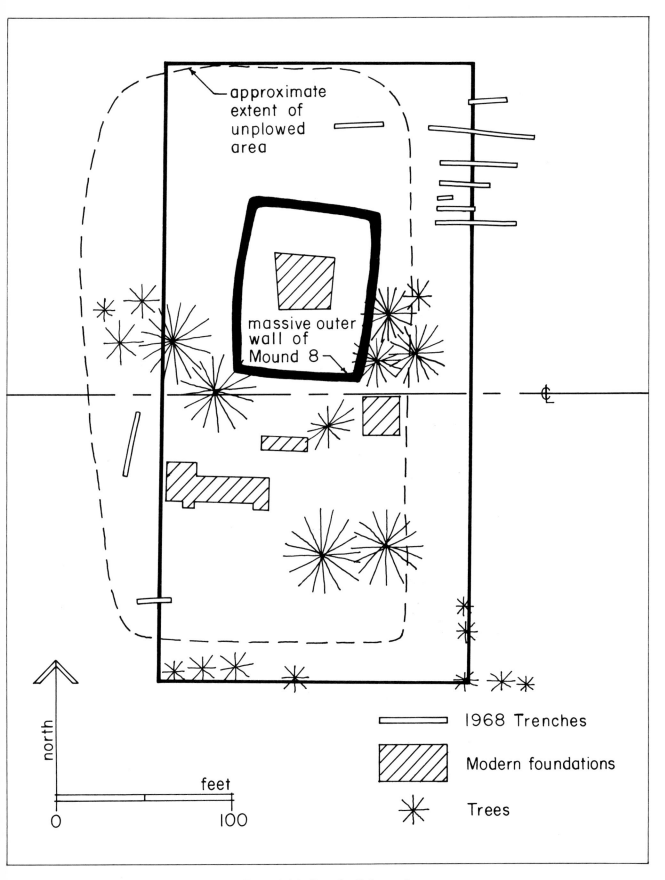

approximate
extent of
unplowed
area

massive outer
wall of
Mound 8

₵

north

feet

0                    100

1968 Trenches

Modern foundations

Trees

*Figure 3.36.* Corridor Sub-area 3.

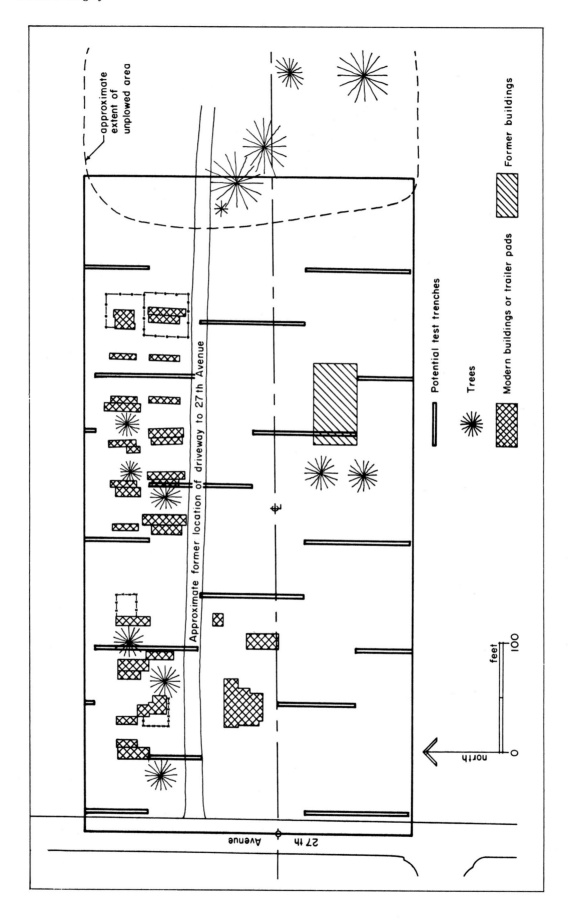

Figure 3.37. Corridor Sub-area 4.

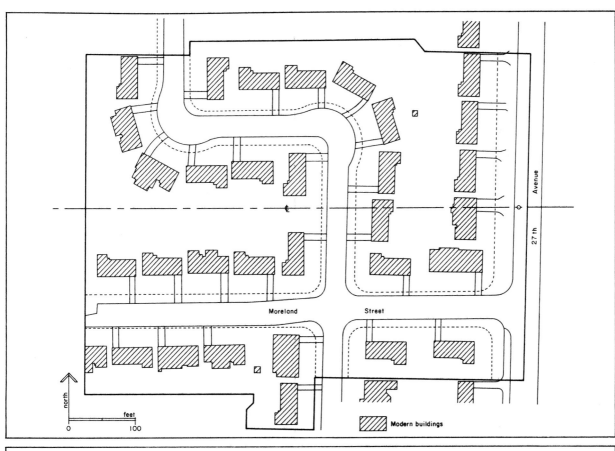

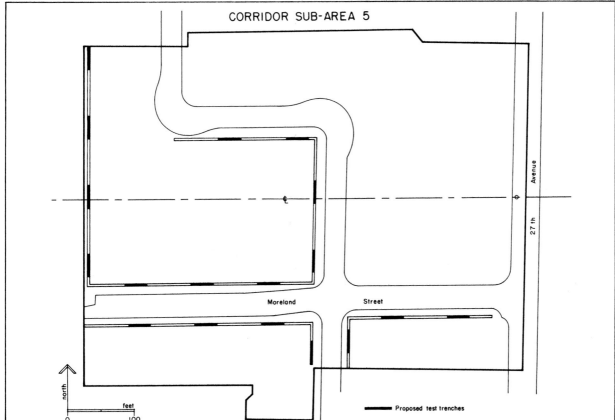

*Figures 3.38 and 3.39.* Corridor Sub-area 5, showing former locations of houses (above) and proposed trenches (below).

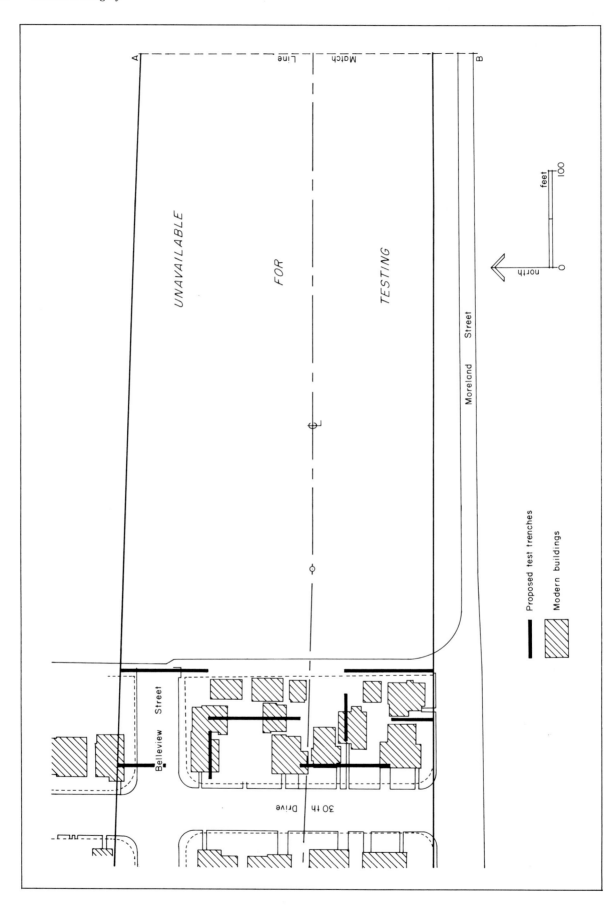

*Figure 3.40 Corridor Sub-area 6.*

trenches in Sub-area 6 will be excavated to a depth of 3 m. The selection of these trenches will be a field decision based on the stratigraphy encountered.

Quantitative data on Sub-area 6 are given below, and include only that portion of the area presently available and targeted for testing.

Area of Sub-area 6: 3992 square meters (1.01 acres)

Area to be covered by proposed trenches: 109.8 square meters

Percentage of area covered by testing: 2.75 percent

## Order of Testing

The order in which the proposed testing will be accomplished is significant in that the information derived from the first areas to be tested may be usefully applied in decisions regarding the subsequent areas dealt with, and in formulating expectations about what may be found here. This is especially true and important for Sub-area 4. Thus the following order will be followed.

Work on sub-areas 1 and 6 will begin first. Since Sub-area 1 is quite large, it may be expected that this work will be in progress for some time. While work in Sub-area 1 is continuing and after completion of work in Sub-area 6, the hand trenching of Sub-area 5 will be started. Upon completion of work in Sub-area 1, the same crew will move into Sub-area 2, which may be expected to be similar to Sub-area 1 in terms of the general stratigraphy represented. Depending on the results of the work in Sub-area 5, and results of the radar survey, in consultation with the SHPO, the work in Sub-area 4 will be accomplished last.

## Summary

The proposed testing outlined above has been structured according to the general goals and purposes stated in the introduction to this document. In addition to addressing the management concerns of providing information on the nature and distribution of subsurface remains within the corridor, the research design presented here delineates some questions that may produce useful and specific scientific information relating to the morphology of Classic period Hohokam sites. The approaches suggested for the successful fulfillment of both management and scientific goals and purposes have been developed within the overriding goal of minimizing any disturbance to the existing resources. This concern has been served through the proposed use of nondestructive testing methods, through the sequential ordering of the testing of the various corridor sub-areas, and through the carefully planned and judicious use of hand excavation and backhoe trenching.

# Appendix

# PLAN OF WORK

The schedule for accomplishing the proposed testing includes a total of 14 weeks (70 working days) and is divided into three phases.

The first phase of the testing will include two weeks of preparatory time, during which briefing and orientation sessions will be held and the basic field logistics worked out. In addition, the end points of the proposed trenches will be surveyed in and staked, and the radar survey accomplished. The Project Director, two crew chiefs, and the consultants will participate in this first phase.

The second phase of the testing includes five weeks of fieldwork. During this time the subsurface testing will be accomplished. The Project Director, two crew chiefs, and 10 crew members will participate in this phase of the work. It is also expected that the consultants will be present part of the time during the fieldwork. The information to be recorded will follow the guidelines outlined above and those stated in the contract. The order of the testing is discussed above.

The third and final phase of the testing will include seven weeks of analysis and write-up time. During this period, the artifacts and nonartifactual samples, profiles, and other relational data recovered during the field testing will be processed and analyzed. The results of the testing will be documented in report form as required by the contract. The Project Director, the two crew chiefs, and the consultants will have the primary responsibilities for the analysis and write-up of the information gained from the testing. In addition, two assistants will be hired for two weeks to assist in the processing of artifactual and nonartifactual materials and samples.

# REFERENCES

Adams, Robert McC., and Hans J. Nissen
1972    *The Uruk Countryside: The Natural Setting of Urban Societies.* Chicago: University of Chicago Press.

Barney, James M.
1931    Sketch map showing some of the earliest homestead entries in the Salt River Valley (copy on file at State Historic Preservation Office, Phoenix).
1933    Phoenix: A history of its pioneer days and people. *Arizona Historical Review* 5(4):264-285.

Bartlett, John Russell
1854    *Personal Narrative of Explorations and Incidents in Texas, New Mexico, California, Sonora, and Chihuahua,* Vol. 2. New York: D. Appleton and Company.

Bluhm, Elaine
1960    Mogollon settlement patterns in Pine Lawn Valley, New Mexico. *American Antiquity* 25(4):538-546.

Bufkin, Don
1977    Phoenix and the Salt River Valley: A cartographer's view. *Journal of Arizona History* 18(3):295-298.

Chang, K.C.
1962    A typology of settlement and community patterns in some circumpolar societies. *Arctic Anthropologist* 1(1):28-41.

Christy, Lloyd B.
1930    *Life History of Colonel William Christy.* Arizona Collection. Tempe: Arizona State University.

Collins, J.H.
1918    A study of marketing conditions in the Salt River Valley, Arizona. *Agricultural Experiment Station Bulletin* 85. Tucson: University of Arizona.

Comstock, Theodore B.
1894    Annual Report to the Board of Regents. In *Arizona Agricultural Experiment Station Bulletin* 1. Tucson: University of Arizona.

Cook, Sherwood F., and Robert F. Heizer
1968    Relationships among houses, settlement areas, and population in aboriginal California. In *Settlement Archaeology,* edited by K.C. Chang. Palo Alto: National Press Books.

Davis, Arthur P.
1897    Irrigation near Phoenix, Arizona. *United States Geological Survey Water Supply and Irrigation Paper* 2. Washington: Government Printing Office.

Doyel, David E.
1974    Excavations in the Escalante Ruin Group. *Arizona State Museum Archaeological Series* 103. Tucson: Arizona State Museum, University of Arizona.
1976    Classic period Hohokam in the Gila River Basin, Arizona. *The Kiva* 42(1):27-37.
1977    Classic period Hohokam in the Escalante Ruin Group. Doctoral dissertation, Department of Anthropology, University of Arizona, Tucson.
1978    Hohokam social organization and the Sedentary to Classic transition. Paper presented at the 43rd Annual Meeting of the Society for American Archaeology, Tucson.

Elliot, W.R., and others
1919    Drainage report, Salt River Valley Water Users' Association. Arizona Collection. Tempe: Arizona State University.

Ezell, Paul H.
1961    The Hispanic acculturation of the Gila River Pimas. *American Anthropological Association Memoir* 90.
1963    The Maricopas: An identification from documentary sources. *Anthropological Papers of the University of Arizona* 6. Tucson: University of Arizona.

Fewkes, Jesse Walter
1909    Prehistoric ruins of the Gila Valley. *Smithsonian Miscellaneous Collections,* Vol. 52. Quarterly Issue 5(4):403-436. Washington: Government Printing Office.
1912    Casa Grande, Arizona. *28th Annual Report of the Bureau of American Ethnology,* 1906-1907, pp. 25-179. Washington: Government Printing Office.

Fowler, B.A.
1904    Salt River Valley Water Users' Association. In F.H. Newel, editor, Proceedings of the First Conference of Engineers of the Reclamation Service, with Accompanying Papers. *United States*

*Water-Supply and Irrigation Paper* 93:130-158. Washington: Government Printing Office.

Frazer, William J.
1959    Changing patterns of land utilitzation within the Salt River Valley of Arizona. Unpublished Doctoral dissertation, Department of Geography, University of Michigan, Ann Arbor.

Fryman, Frank B., Jr., James W. Woodward, Jr., and James W. Garrison
1977    An initial survey of historic resources within the Phoenix metropolitan area, Maricopa County, Arizona. Phoenix: State Historic Preservation Office.

Gumerman, George, and Patricia M. Spoerl
1978    The Hohokam and the northern periphery. Paper presented at the 43rd Annual Meeting of the Society for American Archaeology, Tucson.

Hackenburg, Robert A.
1962    Economic alternatives in arid lands: A case study of the Pima and Papago Indians. *Ethnology* 1:186-195.

Hadley, Elwood
1900    Report of Agent for Pima Agency. *Annual Report of the Department of the Interior, Indian Affairs,* pp. 195-198. Washington: Government Printing Office.

Hammack, Laurens C.
1969    A preliminary report of the excavations at Las Colinas. *The Kiva* 35(1):11-28.

Hammack , Laurens C., and Alan P. Sullivan, editors
1981    The 1968 Excavations at Mound 8 Las Colinas Ruins Group, Phoenix, Arizona. *Arizona State Museum Archaeological Series* 154. Tucson: Arizona State Museum, University of Arizona.

Hammond, Norman
1975    Lubaantun, a classic Maya realm. *Peabody Museum of Archaeology and Ethnology, Monograph* 3. Cambridge.

Harper, W.G., and others
1926    *Soil Survey of the Salt River Valley, Arizona.* United States Department of Agriculture. Bureau of Chemistry and Soils. Washington: Government Printing Office.

Haury, Emil W.
1945    The excavation of Los Muertos and neighboring ruins in the Salt River Valley, southern Arizona. Papers of the *Peabody Museum of American Archaeology and Ethnology* 24(1). Cambridge.
1976    *The Hohokam: Desert Farmers and Craftsmen.* Tucson: University of Arizona Press.

Herskovitz, Robert M.
1974    Arizona U:9:46(ASM)—A Dual Component Hohokam Site in Tempe, Arizona. MS, Arizona State Museum Library, University of Arizona, Tucson.

Hopkins, Ernest J.
1950    *Financing the Frontier: A Fifty Year History of the Valley National Bank, 1899-1949.* Phoenix; Arizona Printers.

Hughes, Thomas Marcus
1971    The politics of water resource management in the Phoenix metropolitan area. Unpublished Doctoral dissertation, Department of Geography, University of Arizona, Tucson.

Kent, Edward
1910    Patrick T. Hurley versus Charles F. Abbott and others. Decision and Decree, filed March 1, 1910. Phoenix: Salt River Valley Water Users' Association.

Lee, Willis T.
1905    Underground water of Salt River Valley, Arizona. *United States*

McClatchie, Alfred J.
1901    Irrigation at the Station Farm, 1898-1901. *Arizona Agricultural Experiment Station Bulletin* 41. Tucson: University of Arizona.
1902    Utilizing our water supply. *Arizona Agricultural Experiment Station Bulletin* 43. Tucson: University of Arizona.

McClatchie, Alfred J., and Robert H. Forbes
1899    Sugar beet experiments during 1898. *Arizona Agricultural Experiment Station Bulletin* 30. Tucson: University of Arizona.
        Geological Survey Water-Supply and Irrigation Paper 136. Washington.
        Maricopa County Immigration Union
1887    *What the Salt River Valley Offers to the Immigrant, Capitalist, and Invalid.* Chicago: Rand, McNally.

Masse, W. Bruce
1976    The Hohokam expressway project: A study of prehistoric irrigation in the Salt River Valley. *Contributions to Highway Salvage Archaeology in Arizona* 43. Tucson: Arizona State Museum, University of Arizona.

Matlock, R.L., and S.P. Clark
1934    Production costs and returns from major Salt River Valley field crops 1928-1930. *Arizona Agricultural Experiment Station Bulletin* 146. Tucson: University of Arizona.

Mawn, Geoffrey P.
1977    Promoters, speculators, and the selection of the Phoenix townsite. *Arizona and the West* 19(3):207-224.

Means, Thomas H.
1902    Soil survey of the Salt River Valley. *Arizona Agricultural Experiment Station Bulletin* 40. Tucson: University of Arizona.

Meggers, Betty J., editor
1955    Functional and evolutionary implications of community patterning. In *Memoirs of the Society*

*for American Archaeology*, Robert Wauchope, editor Salt Lake City.

Midvale, Frank
n.d. Unpublished notes. MS, The Frank Midvale Collection, Department of Anthropology, Arizona State University, Tempe.

Moorehead, Warren K.
1906 A narrative of explorations in New Mexico, Arizona, Indiana, etc. *Bulletin 3, Phillips Academy Department of Archaeology*. Andover.

Morris, Donald H. and Mahmoud El-Najjar
1971 An unusual Classic period burial from Las Colinas, Salt River Valley, central Arizona. *The Kiva* 36(4):30-35.

Nelson, Reuben
1981 Twelve years of surveying, monitoring, and excavating the La Ciudad de los Hornos site. MS on file, Arizona State Museum, University of Arizona, Tucson.

Parsons, Lee A.
1972 Archaeological settlement patterns. In *Annual Review of Anthropology, 1972*. Palo Alto: Annual Reviews.

Patrick, H.R.
1903 The ancient canal systems and pueblos of the Salt River Valley. *Phoenix Free Museum Bulletin* 1. Phoenix.

Peplow, Edward H., Jr.
1979 *The Taming of the Salt: A Collection of Biographies of Pioneers who Contributed Significantly to Water Development in the Salt River Valley*. Phoenix: Salt River Project (second printing).

Phoenix Daily Herald Office
1886 Maricopa County, Arizona. Reliable Information on the Splendid Opportunities it Offers to Settlers. Special Collections, University of Arizona Library.

Plog, Fred T.
1974 Settlement patterns and social history. in *Frontiers of Anthropology* edited by Murray Leaf. New York: Van Nostrand.
1978 Explaining culture change in the Hohokam preclassic. Paper presented at the 43rd Annual Meeting of the Society for American Archaeology, Tucson.

Roberts, Michael E.
in press Subsurface radar and prehistoric sites: Report on a pilot study. In *Radar in Archaeology*, edited by P. Pratt. New York: Academic Press.

Russell, Frank
1975 *The Pima Indians*. Tucson: University of Arizona Press.

Schroeder, Albert H.
1953 The bearing of architecture on developments in the Hohokam Classic period. *Southwestern Journal of Anthropology* 9:174-194.

Smith, Courtland L.
1972 *The Salt River Project: A Case Study in Adaptation to an Urbanizing Community*. Tucson: University of Arizona Press.

Spier, Leslie
1933 *Yuman Tribes of the Gila River*. Chicago: University of Chicago Press.

Staski, Edward
1981 The historic materials from Las Colinas. MS, Arizona State Museum, University of Arizona, Tucson.

Struever, Stuart
1968 Woodland subsistence and settlement systems in the lower Illinois Valley. In *New Perspectives in Archaeology*, edited by Sally R. Binford and Lewis R. Binford. Chicago: Aldine.

Teague, Lynn S.
1981 Test excavations at Painted Rock Reservoir: sites AZ Z:1:7, AZ Z:1:8, and AZ S:16:36. *Arizona State Museum Archaeological Series* 143. Tucson: Arizona State Museum, University of Arizona.